A Great Man

Teacher's Guide

Unit 21

Note: See New and Important Objectives on page 2 for a complete list of skills taught and reviewed.

Critical Foundations in Primary Reading

Marilyn Sprick, Ann Watanabe, Karen Akiyama-Paik, and Shelley V. Jones

Sopris West®
EDUCATIONAL SERVICES

A Cambium Learning® Company

BOSTON, MA • LONGMONT, CO

ISBN 13 digit: 978-1-60218-544-9
ISBN 10-digit: 1-60218-544-1

7 8 9 10 11 B&B 16 15 14 13 12

167046/6-12

Table of Contents
Unit 21
A Great Man

How to Teach the Lessons

End of the Unit

Read Well 2 Sequence and Sound Pronunciation Guide

Letter Sounds and Combinations

Cumulative Review of *Read Well 1* Sounds and Combinations (Ss, Ee, ee, Mm, Aa, Dd, th, Nn, Tt, Ww, Ii, Th, Hh, Cc, Rr, ea, sh, Sh, Kk, -ck, oo, ar, wh, Wh, ĕ, -y as in fly, Ll, Oo, Bb, all, Gg, Ff, Uu, er, oo as in book, Yy, a schwa, Pp, ay, Vv, Qq, Jj, Xx, or, Zz, a_e, -y as in baby, i_e, ou, ow as in cow, ch, Ch, ai, igh, o_e, ir) and:

Unit 2	Unit 3			Unit 5	Unit 6
aw	ew	ue	u_e	ow	ge
/aw/	/o͞o/	/o͞o/	/o͞o/	/ōōō/	/j/
Paw	**Crew**	**Blue**	**Flute**	**Snow**	**Page**
Voiced	Voiced	Voiced	Bossy E Voiced	Voiced (Long)	Voiced
Unit 6	**Unit 7**		**Unit 8**		**Unit 10**
-dge	ci	ce	kn	ph	oa
/j/	/sss/	/sss/	/nnn/	/fff/	/ōōō/
Badge	**Circle**	**Center**	**Knee**	**Phone**	**Boat**
Voiced	Unvoiced	Unvoiced	Voiced	Unvoiced	Voiced (Long)
Unit 11		**Unit 12**		**Unit 13**	
oi	ea	gi	au	oy	
/oi/	/ĕĕĕ/	/j/	/au/	/oy/	
Point	**Bread**	**Giraffe**	**Astronaut**	**Boy**	
Voiced	Voiced (Short)	Voiced	Voiced	Voiced	

Affixes (including morphographs—affixes taught with meaning) and Open Syllables

Cumulative Review of *Read Well 1* Affixes (-ed, -en, -es, -ing, -ly, -s, -y, -tion) and:

Unit 2	Unit 3		Unit 5		Unit 6
re-	un-	ex-	o	-ful	bi-
Means again as in reread	**Means not** as in unhappy	as in excited	Open syllable /ō/ as in open and moment	**Means full of** as in colorful	**Means two** as in bicycle
Unit 7	**Unit 8**	**Unit 11**	**Unit 12**	**Unit 13**	
de-	-able	i	be-	-ous	dis-
as in detective	as in comfortable	Open syllable /ī/ as in silence and pilot	as in before	as in enormous	as in discover
Unit 14		**Unit 15**		**Unit 16**	
-al	-ible	-or	-ment	-ic	pre-
as in animal	as in flexible	**Means one who** as in actor	as in apartment	as in scientific	**Means before** as in preview
Unit 17		**Unit 18**		**Unit 19**	
-ity	-sion	-ness	-less	in-	im-
as in activity	as in permission	as in fairness	**Means without** as in helpless	as in insert	**Means not** as in impossible

Introduction
A Great Man

Story Notes

The 16th President: How did a poor boy from a poor family become one of the most esteemed presidents the United States has ever had? This biography of Abraham Lincoln describes his lifelong love of learning and determination to succeed. The historical narrative also discusses the major political and social issues facing the United States at a critical time in its history. We hope your students enjoy this inspiring story about how one person can make a difference for many.

Changing the Face of History: In this unit's fluency passage, students will be surprised at how a little girl's suggestion changed the face of history.

> **CAUTION**
> **(Reminder)**
> Do not read the Read Aloud recommendations during small group instruction. Reserve this time for students to read.

Recommended Read Alouds

The *Read Well 2* suggested Read Alouds enhance small group instruction—providing opportunities to further build background knowledge and vocabulary.

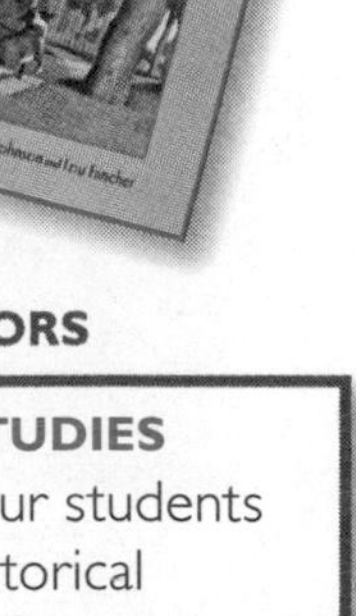

Sweet Clara and the Freedom Quilt by Deborah Hopkinson
Fiction • Historical Narrative
In the darkness of the night, using a mysterious map that can be read by only a secretive few, a young girl on a plantation guides many slaves to freedom. This inspiring story gives your students a glimpse into a time in our nation's past and into the acts of courage that made a difference for many.

The Boy on Fairfield Street by Kathleen Krull
Nonfiction • Biography
Find out how the creator of the Cat in the Hat got his start by breaking the rules and getting voted "Least Likely to Succeed" by his classmates.

Read Well Connections
Students will gain greater insight into slavery and the conflicts that led up to the Civil War in *Sweet Clara and the Freedom Quilt. The Boy on Fairfield Street* is another biography of an inspiring person who went on to great success as an author and illustrator.

NOTE FROM THE AUTHORS

> **CONNECTIONS: SOCIAL STUDIES**
> You will be amazed at how well your students will grasp the significance of the historical events and people in this unit. The foundational content knowledge in American history will prepare them well for understanding concepts they will encounter in the upper grades. Your students are learning more and more each day!

New and Important Objectives

A Research-Based Reading Program

Phonemic Awareness
Phonics
Fluency
Vocabulary
Comprehension

Phonics

Cumulative Letter Sounds and Combinations

Review • Ss, Ee, ee, Mm, Aa, Dd, th, Nn, Tt, Ww, Ii, Th, Hh, Cc, Rr, ea, sh, Sh, Kk, -ck, oo, ar, wh, Wh, ĕ, -y (as in fly), Ll, Oo, Bb, all, Gg, Ff, Uu, er, oo (as in book), Yy, a (schwa), Pp, ay, Vv, Qq, Jj, Xx, or, Zz, a_e, -y (as in baby), i_e, ou, ow (as in cow), ch, Ch, ai, igh, o_e, ir, aw, ew, ue, u_e, ow (as in snow), ge, -dge, ci, ce, kn, ph, oa, oi, ea (as in bread), gi, au, oy

Cumulative Affixes, Morphographs, and Open Syllables

Review • -ed, -en, -er, -es, -est, -ing, -ly, -s, -y, -tion, re-, un-, ex-, o (as in open), -ful, bi-, de-, -able, i (as in silence), be-, -ous, dis-, -al, -ible, -or, -ment, -ic, pre-, -ity, -sion, -ness, -less, in-, im-

★New Proper Nouns

Abe ◆ Abraham Lincoln, Abraham's, Bible, Civil War, February, George Washington, Grace Bedell, Grace's, Illinois, John Wilkes Booth, Joshua, Kentucky, Lincoln Memorial, Lincoln's, Lincolns, Mary Todd, Mr. Lincoln, Mr. Lincoln's, Nancy Hanks, New Orleans, New Salem, November ◆ October, Ohio, Sarah Bush Johnston, Sarah Thomas Lincoln, White House, Washington, D.C.

★New Pattern Words

◆ axe, flag ◆ ill, law, laws, plow, plump, rest, snuck ◆ stump, thrilled, vote, voted, votes, voting

*__Known Pattern Words With Affixes__ • beings, buildable, fished, hated, hoping, joined, joyful, owned, owning, pants, precooked, roads, shocked, speeches

★New Compound and Hyphenated Words

bearskin, beehive, birthplace, cornhusks ◆ fireplace, flatboat, gentleman, kind-hearted, lawmaker, re-elected, saddlebags ◆ stepmother

* **Known Pattern Words With Affixes**, **Known Tricky Words With Affixes**, and **Known Multisyllabic Words With Affixes** have base words students have previously read. The words are new in this unit because they have not been previously read with the affix.

★ = New in this unit

◆ = Words that are not introduced in the exercises before they are read in the storybook

Phonics *(continued)*

★Other New Multisyllabic Words

admit, afford, aloud, balcony ◆ cabin, capital, congregation, copy, elect, elected, election, furniture, general, holiday, image, imitate, imitated, inspire, inspired, lawyer, married, marry, mattresses, memorial, nation's, nations, opinion, opinions, peddlers, platform, preacher, preacher's, preachers, president, presidents, remarried, remarry ◆ slavery, speakers, surrender, surrendered, swollen, theater, transport, voter, voters, whiskers

*__Known Multisyllabic Words With Affixes__ • bicoastal, husbands, ladies, littles, markets, numbers, parents', photographed, regularity, rescued

★New Tricky Words

cousin, encourage, encouraged, fought, honor, opinion, statue, territories

*__Known Tricky Words With Affixes__ • believed, fields, movable, received, schooling, watchful

Fluency

Accuracy, Expression, Phrasing, Rate

Vocabulary

New • educated, encourage, expensive, government, imitate, impressive, inspire, inspiring, opinion, slave, slavery, surrender, towering, transport

Review • adventure, allow, approximately, bittersweet, common, courage, experiment, immigrant, ordinary, permission, pioneer, respect, responsible, slave, survive, trader, widow

Reviewed in Context • adventure, advice, allow, amazed, belongings, bittersweet, caption, community, courage, glimpse, impressed, integrity, local, locate, neighborhood, ordinary, organize, perfect, pioneer, plain, respect, settler, spunky, survive, thrilled, trader, victory, wealthy, widow

Comprehension

Unit Genres

Nonfiction • Biography

Nonfiction • Historical Narrative

Comprehension Processes

Build Knowledge: Factual, Procedural, Conceptual

Day	1	2	3	4	5	6
Remember						
Defining						
Identifying (recalling)	S,C	S	S		S	E
Using						
Understand						
Defining (in your own words)	C	S	S		S	E,C
Describing			S	C		C
Explaining (rephrasing)	S	S	S,C	S	S	S
Illustrating						
Sequencing						E
Summarizing	C	S,C	S,C	S,C	S	E
Using	S	S	S,C	S	S	E,C
Visualizing	S	S				
Apply						
Demonstrating						
Explaining (unstated)	S	S	S	S,C	S,C	E,S
Illustrating						
Inferring	S,C	S	S	S,C	S,C	S
Making Connections (relating)					S	
Predicting				S		
Using	S	S	S,C	S,C	S	S
Analyze						
Classifying						
Comparing/Contrasting		S	S			
Distinguishing Cause/Effect						C
Drawing Conclusions	S	S		S	S	E,S
Inferring						
Evaluate						
Making Judgments	S	S				
Responding (personal)		S			S,C	
Create						
Generating Ideas	S,C	S,C	C	C	S,C	S,C

E = Exercise, S = Storybook, C = Comprehension & Skill

Comprehension *(continued)*

Skills and Strategies

Day	1	2	3	4	5	6
Priming Background Knowledge	S			S		E
Setting a Purpose for Reading	S	S	S			
Answering Questions	S	S	S	S	S	S
Asking Questions	S,C					C
Visualizing	S	S				
Comprehension Monitoring/Fix Ups						
Does it Make Sense?	C	C	C	C		
Looking Back						
Restating						
Summarizing						
Main Idea						
Retelling						
Supporting Details	C	C	C	C		
Understanding Text Structure						
Title, Author, Illustrator	S,C	S	S	S		
Fact or Fiction						
Genre (Classifying)	S,C	S				
Narrative						
Setting	S					
Main Character/Traits (Characterization)			S	S,C		C
Goal						
Problem/Solution						
Action/Events/Sequence						E
Outcome/Conclusion						
Lesson/Author's Message						
Expository						
Subject/Topic						
Heading						
Supporting Details (Facts/Information)	C	C	C	C		
Main Idea						
Using Graphic Organizers						
Chart						
Diagram (labeling)						
Hierarchy (topic/detail)						
K-W-L						
Map (locating, labeling)				S		
Matrix (compare/contrast)						C
Sequence (linear, cycle, cause and effect)			C			E
Story Map						
Web				C		C

E = Exercise, S = Storybook, C = Comprehension & Skill

Comprehension *(continued)*

Study Skills

Day	1	2	3	4	5	6
Alphabetical Order						
Following Directions						
Locating Information	C	S,C	S,C			
Note Taking						
Previewing						
Reviewing		S	S	S	S	
Test Taking		C				C
Using Glossary		S	S			
Using Table of Contents	S					
Viewing	S,C	S,C	C	C	C	
Verifying						

Writing in Response to Reading

Day	1	2	3	4	5	6
Sentence Completion	C	C	C	C	C	C
Making Lists	C	C				
Sentence Writing	C	C	C	C	C	C
Story Retell/Summary						
Fact Summary	C	C	C	C		
Paragraph Writing	C	C	C	C	C	C
Report Writing						
Open-Ended Response					C	
Creative Writing					C	

Writing Traits

(Addressed within the context of Writing in Response to Reading)

Day	1	2	3	4	5	6
Ideas and Content						
Elaborating/Generating	C	C	C	C	C	
Organization						
Introduction						
Topic Sentence						
Supporting Details						
Sequencing						
Word Choice						
Sophisticated Words (Tier 2 and 3)	C	C	C	C	C	C
Conventions						
Capital	C	C	C	C	C	C
Ending Punctuation	C	C	C	C	C	C
Other (commas, quotation marks)						
Presentation						
Handwriting	C	C	C	C	C	C
Neatness	C	C	C	C	C	C

E = Exercise, S = Storybook, C = Comprehension & Skill

Daily Lesson Planning

LESSON PLAN FORMAT

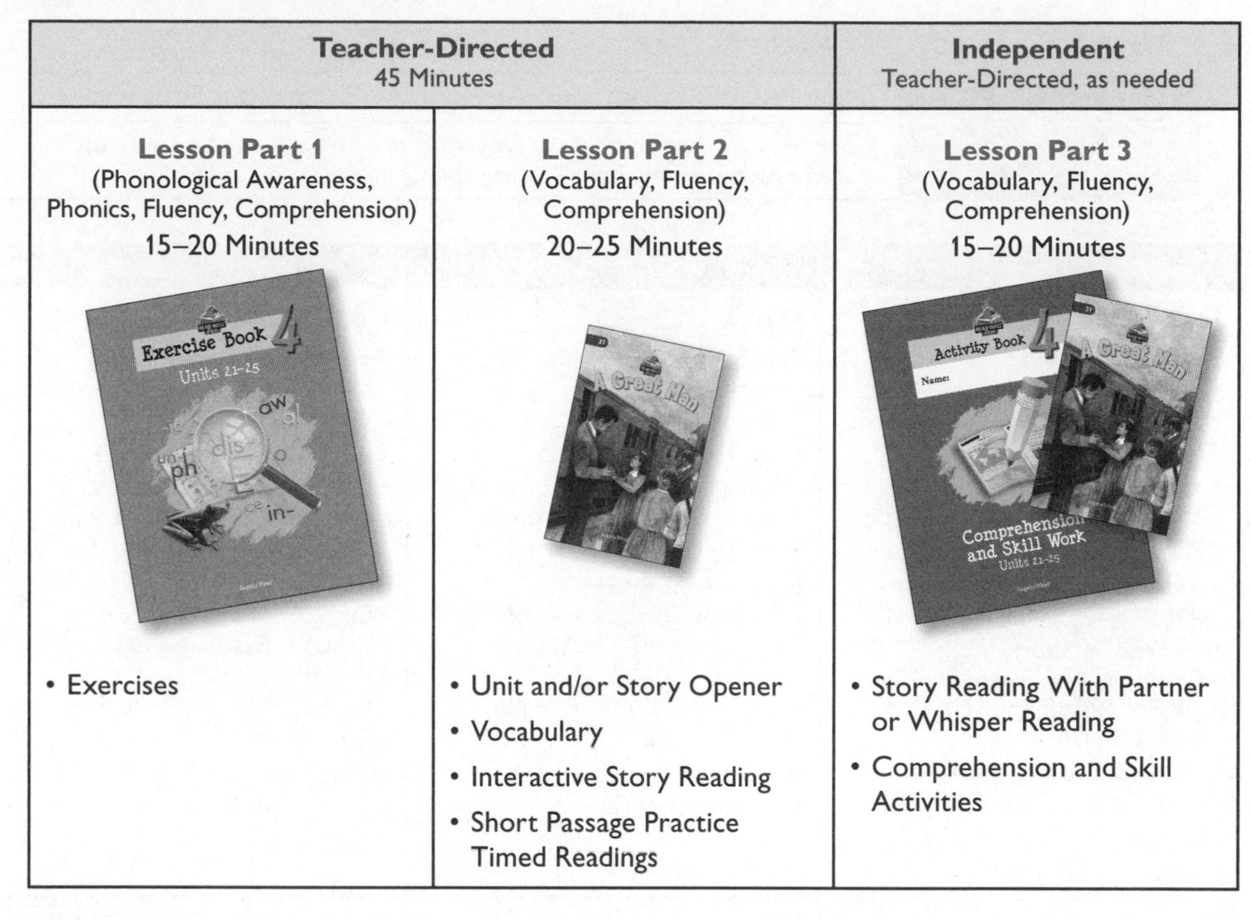

Teacher-Directed 45 Minutes		Independent Teacher-Directed, as needed
Lesson Part 1 (Phonological Awareness, Phonics, Fluency, Comprehension) 15–20 Minutes	**Lesson Part 2** (Vocabulary, Fluency, Comprehension) 20–25 Minutes	**Lesson Part 3** (Vocabulary, Fluency, Comprehension) 15–20 Minutes
• Exercises	• Unit and/or Story Opener • Vocabulary • Interactive Story Reading • Short Passage Practice Timed Readings	• Story Reading With Partner or Whisper Reading • Comprehension and Skill Activities

HOMEWORK

Read Well Homework (blackline masters of new *Read Well 2* passages) provides an opportunity for children to celebrate accomplishments with parents. Homework should be sent home on routine days.

ORAL READING FLUENCY ASSESSMENT

Upon completion of this unit, assess each student and proceed to Unit 22, as appropriate.

WRITTEN ASSESSMENT

During the time students would normally complete Comprehension and Skill Activities, students will be administered a Written Assessment that can be found on page 93 in the students' *Activity Book 4*.

Note: See Making Decisions for additional assessment information.

EXTENDING PLANS

Two plans illustrate how to use materials for students with various learning needs. As you set up your unit plan, always include *Read Well 2 Plus* Exercises and Story Reading on a daily basis. Unit 21 includes 6- and 8-Day Plans.

Plans	For groups that:
6-DAY	Complete Oral Reading Fluency Assessments with Passes and Strong Passes
8-DAY	Complete Oral Reading Fluency Assessments with Passes and require teacher-guided assistance with Story Reading and Comprehension and Skill Work

<table>
<tr><th colspan="3">6-DAY PLAN</th></tr>
<tr>
<td>Day 1
Teacher-Directed
• Exercise 1
• Unit and Story Opener: A Great Man, The 16th President
• Vocabulary, Ch. 1
• The 16th President, Introduction
• Guide practice, as needed, on Comp & Skill 1, Lincoln Mini-Book Cover, Entry 1
Independent Work
• On Your Own: Partner or Whisper Read, The 16th President, Ch. 1
• Comp & Skill 1, Lincoln Mini-Book Cover, Entry 1
Homework
• Homework Passage 1</td>
<td>Day 2
Teacher-Directed
• Exercise 2
• Vocabulary, Ch. 2, 3
• The 16th President, Ch. 2
• Guide practice, as needed, on Comp & Skill 2, and preview Lincoln Mini-Book Entry 2
Independent Work
• On Your Own: Partner or Whisper Read, The 16th President, Ch. 3
• Comp & Skill 2, Lincoln Mini-Book Entry 2
Homework
• Homework Passage 2</td>
<td>Day 3
Teacher-Directed
• Exercise 3
• Vocabulary, Ch. 4–6
• The 16th President, Ch. 4
• Guide practice, as needed, on Comp & Skill 3, and preview Lincoln Mini-Book Entry 3
Independent Work
• On Your Own: Partner or Whisper Read, The 16th President, Ch. 5
• Comp & Skill 3, Lincoln Mini-Book Entry 3
Homework
• Homework Passage 3</td>
</tr>
<tr>
<td>Day 4
Teacher-Directed
• Exercise 4
• The 16th President, Ch. 6
• Guide practice, as needed, on Comp & Skill Extra Fluency Passage (optional), Comp & Skill 4, Lincoln Mini-Book Entry 4
Independent Work
• Repeated Reading: Partner or Whisper Read, The 16th President, Ch. 6
• Comp & Skill 4, Lincoln Mini-Book Entry 4, Extra Fluency Passage (optional)
Homework
• Homework Passage 4</td>
<td>Day 5
Teacher-Directed
• Exercise 5
• Vocabulary, Ch. 7
• The 16th President, Ch. 7
• Preview Lincoln Mini-Book Entries 5a, 5b and guide practice, as needed, on Comp & Skill Just for Fun (optional)
Independent Work
• Repeated Reading: Partner or Whisper Read, The 16th President, Ch. 7
• Lincoln Mini-Book Entries 5a and 5b, Comp & Skill Just for Fun (optional)
Homework
• Homework Passage 5</td>
<td>Day 6
Teacher-Directed
• Exercise 6a
• Exercise 6b: Focus Lesson
• Fluency, Changing the Face of History
Independent Work
• Repeated Reading: Partner or Whisper Read, Changing the Face of History
• Written Assessment
• Oral Reading Fluency Assessment*
Homework
• Homework Passage 6</td>
</tr>
</table>

Note: Unit 21 features an extra Just for Fun Comp & Skill activity (see page 83 in this guide). This page can be used any time during the unit.

* The Oral Reading Fluency Assessments are individually administered by the teacher while students are working on their Written Assessments.

8-DAY PLAN			
Day 1 **Teacher-Directed** • Exercise 1 • Unit and Story Opener: A Great Man, The 16th President • Vocabulary, Ch. 1 • The 16th President, Introduction • Guide practice, as needed, on Comp & Skill 1, Lincoln Mini-Book Cover, Entry 1 **Independent Work** • On Your Own: Partner or Whisper Read, The 16th President, Ch. 1 • Comp & Skill 1, Lincoln Mini-Book Cover, Entry 1 **Homework** • Homework Passage 1	**Day 2** **Teacher-Directed** • Exercise 2 • Vocabulary, Ch. 2, 3 • The 16th President, Ch. 2 • Guide practice, as needed, on Comp & Skill 2 **Independent Work** • Repeated Reading: Partner or Whisper Read, The 16th President, Ch. 2 • Comp & Skill 2 **Homework** • Homework Passage 2	**Day 3** **Teacher-Directed** • Review Exercise 2 • Review Vocabulary, Ch. 2, 3 • The 16th President, Ch. 3 • Guide practice, as needed, on Lincoln Mini-Book Entry 2 **Independent Work** • Repeated Reading: Partner or Whisper Read, The 16th President, Ch. 3 • Lincoln Mini-Book Entry 2 **Homework** • Teacher's Choice	**Day 4** **Teacher-Directed** • Exercise 3 • Vocabulary, Ch. 4–6 • The 16th President, Ch. 4 • Guide practice, as needed, on Comp & Skill 3 **Independent Work** • Repeated Reading: Partner or Whisper Read, The 16th President, Ch. 4 • Comp & Skill 3 **Homework** • Homework Passage 3
Day 5 **Teacher-Directed** • Review Exercise 3 • Review Vocabulary, Ch. 4–6 • The 16th President, Ch. 5 • Guide practice, as needed, on Comp & Skill Extra Fluency Passage, Lincoln Mini-Book Entry 3 **Independent Work** • Repeated Reading: Partner or Whisper Read, The 16th President, Ch. 5 • Comp & Skill Extra Fluency Passage, Lincoln Mini-Book Entry 3 **Homework** • Teacher's Choice	**Day 6** **Teacher-Directed** • Exercise 4 • The 16th President, Ch. 6 • Guide practice, as needed, on Comp & Skill 4, Lincoln Mini-Book Entry 4 **Independent Work** • Repeated Reading: Partner or Whisper Read, The 16th President, Ch. 6 • Comp & Skill 4, Lincoln Mini-Book Entry 4 **Homework** • Homework Passage 4	**Day 7** **Teacher-Directed** • Exercise 5 • Vocabulary, Ch. 7 • The 16th President, Ch. 7 • Guide practice, as needed, on Lincoln Mini-Book Entries 5a and 5b, Comp & Skill Just for Fun (optional) **Independent Work** • Repeated Reading: Partner or Whisper Read, The 16th President, Ch. 7 • Lincoln Mini-Book Entries 5a and 5b, Comp & Skill Just for Fun (optional) **Homework** • Homework Passage 5	**Day 8** **Teacher-Directed** • Exercise 6a • Exercise 6b: Focus Lesson • Fluency, Changing the Face of History **Independent Work** • Repeated Reading: Partner or Whisper Read, Changing the Face of History • Written Assessment • Oral Reading Fluency Assessment* **Homework** • Homework Passage 6

Materials and Materials Preparation

Core Lessons

Teacher Materials

***READ WELL 2* MATERIALS**

- Unit 21 Teacher's Guide
- Sound Cards
- Unit 21 Oral Reading Fluency Assessment found on page 101
- Group Assessment Record found in the *Assessment Manual*

SCHOOL SUPPLIES

Stopwatch or watch with a second hand

Student Materials

***READ WELL 2* MATERIALS (for each student)**

- *A Great Man* storybook
- *Exercise Book 4*
- *Activity Book 4* or copies of Unit 21 Comprehension and Skill Work
- Unit 21 Written Assessment found in *Activity Book 4*, page 93, and on the blackline master CD.
- Unit 21 Certificate of Achievement (BLM, page 102)
- Unit 21 Homework (blackline masters)
  See *Getting Started* for suggested homework routines.

SCHOOL SUPPLIES

Pencils, colors (optional—markers, crayons, or colored pencils), highlighters

Make one copy per student of each blackline master, as appropriate for the group.

Note: For new or difficult Comprehension and Skill Activities, make overhead transparencies from the blackline masters. Use the transparencies to demonstrate and guide practice.

FOCUS LESSON

For Exercise 6b (Focus Lesson), make overhead transparencies from the blackline masters, write on transparencies placed over the pages, or use paper copies to demonstrate how to complete the lessons.

SPECIAL NOTE

Your students will complete a mini-book. For ease of use, pull pages 1–4 from *Activity Book 4* or make double-sided copies of the BLMs. Staple the pages down the center to create a mini-book.

How to Teach the Lessons

Teach from this section. Each instructional component is outlined in an easy-to-teach format.

Exercise 1

- Unit and Story Opener: A Great Man, The 16th President
- Vocabulary
- Story Reading 1
  With the Teacher: Introduction
  On Your Own: Chapter 1
- Comp and Skill Activity 1, Lincoln Mini-Book Cover, Entry 1

Exercise 2

- Vocabulary
- Story Reading 2
  With the Teacher: Chapter 2
  On Your Own: Chapter 3
- Comp and Skill Activity 2, Lincoln Mini-Book Entry 2

Exercise 3

- Vocabulary
- Story Reading 3
  With the Teacher: Chapter 4
  On Your Own: Chapter 5
- Comp and Skill Activity 3, Lincoln Mini-Book Entry 3

Exercise 4

- Story Reading 4
  With the Teacher: Chapter 6
- Comp and Skill Activity 4, Lincoln Mini-Book Entry 4

Exercise 5

- Vocabulary
- Story Reading 5
  With the Teacher: Chapter 7
- Mini-Book Entries 5a, 5b

Exercise 6a

- Exercise 6b, Focus Lesson: Timeline
- Story Reading 6
  With the Teacher: Changing the Face of History (Fluency)
- Written Assessment

Note: Lessons include daily homework.

> **PACING**
> Exercise 1 should take about 15 minutes.

❶ SOUND REVIEW

Have students read the sounds and key word phrases. Work for accuracy, then fluency.

❷ SOUND PRACTICE

- For each task, have students spell and say the focus sound in the gray bar. For Bossy E, read the header.
- Next, have students read each underlined sound, the word, then the whole column.
- Repeat with each column, building accuracy first, then fluency.

❸ ACCURACY AND FLUENCY BUILDING

- For each task, have students say any underlined part, then read the word.
- Set a pace. Then have students read the whole words in each task and column.
- Provide repeated practice, building accuracy first, then fluency.

C1, D1. Rhyming Words

Have students read the words and identify what's the same about them.

E1. Tricky Words

For each Tricky Word, have students use the sounds and word parts they know to silently sound out the word. Use the word in a sentence to help with pronunciation.

honor

Look at the first word. The h is silent. Read the word. (honor) When you show your respect for someone, you . . . *honor* . . . them. Read the word two times. (honor, honor)

statue

Look at the next word. It's tricky, but I think you can read it. Use my sentence to help you with the pronunciation. When you are tagged during a game of Freeze, you have to stand as still as a . . . statue. Read the word three times. (statue, statue, statue)

whose Zeke found a jacket, but he doesn't know . . . *whose* . . . it is.
died Jade was sad when her pet fish . . . *died.*
country The United States of America is a . . . *country.*
warmed The soup was cold, so we . . . *warmed* . . . it up.

❹ MULTISYLLABIC WORDS

For each word, have students read the syllables, then the whole word. Use the word in a sentence, as appropriate.

Bible Many people practice the lessons taught in a book called the . . . *Bible.*
president George Washington was America's first . . . *president.*
mattresses The kids at camp had a hard time sleeping on the lumpy . . . *mattresses.*
capital Washington, D.C., is the nation's . . . *capital.*

❺ NAMES AND PLACES

- Tell students these are people and places they will read about in the story.
- Have students use the sounds and word parts they know to figure out the words. Use the words in sentences, as needed.

6 GENERALIZATION: READING NEW WORDS IN PARAGRAPHS

Have students read the paragraph silently, then out loud. Tell students to use the sounds and word parts they know to read any difficult words.

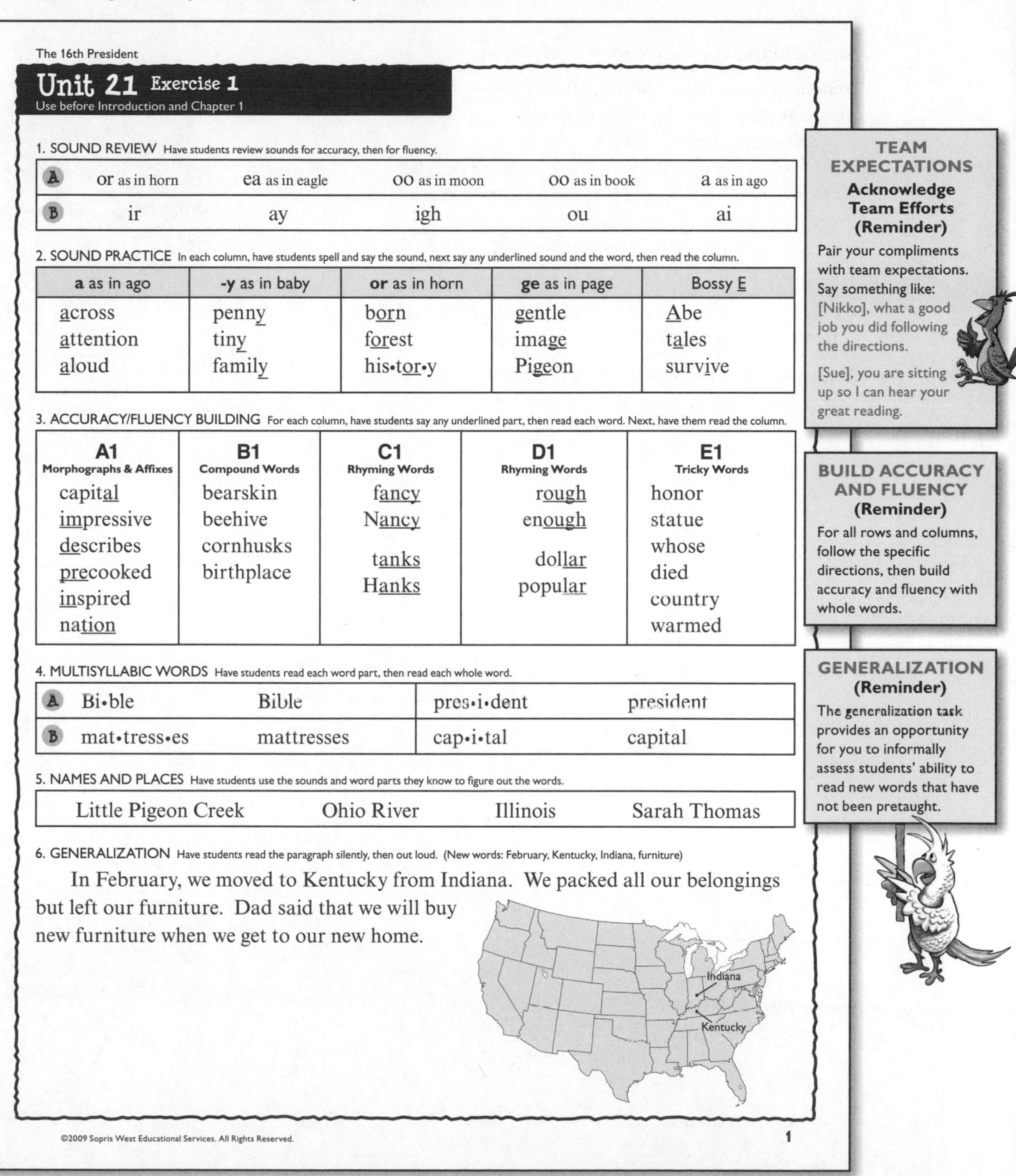

The 16th President

Unit 21 Exercise 1

Use before Introduction and Chapter 1

1. SOUND REVIEW Have students review sounds for accuracy, then for fluency.

A	or as in horn	ea as in eagle	oo as in moon	oo as in book	a as in ago
B	ir	ay	igh	ou	ai

2. SOUND PRACTICE In each column, have students spell and say the sound, next say any underlined sound and the word, then read the column.

a as in ago	-y as in baby	or as in horn	ge as in page	Bossy E
across	penny	born	gentle	Abe
attention	tiny	forest	image	tales
aloud	family	his•tor•y	Pigeon	survive

3. ACCURACY/FLUENCY BUILDING For each column, have students say any underlined part, then read each word. Next, have them read the column.

A1 Morphographs & Affixes	B1 Compound Words	C1 Rhyming Words	D1 Rhyming Words	E1 Tricky Words
capital	bearskin	fancy	rough	honor
impressive	beehive	Nancy	enough	statue
describes	cornhusks	tanks	dollar	whose
precooked	birthplace	Hanks	popular	died
inspired				country
nation				warmed

4. MULTISYLLABIC WORDS Have students read each word part, then read each whole word.

A	Bi•ble	Bible	pres•i•dent	president
B	mat•tress•es	mattresses	cap•i•tal	capital

5. NAMES AND PLACES Have students use the sounds and word parts they know to figure out the words.

Little Pigeon Creek	Ohio River	Illinois	Sarah Thomas

6. GENERALIZATION Have students read the paragraph silently, then out loud. (New words: February, Kentucky, Indiana, furniture)

In February, we moved to Kentucky from Indiana. We packed all our belongings but left our furniture. Dad said that we will buy new furniture when we get to our new home.

1

TEAM EXPECTATIONS

Acknowledge Team Efforts (Reminder)

Pair your compliments with team expectations. Say something like:

[Nikko], what a good job you did following the directions.

[Sue], you are sitting up so I can hear your great reading.

BUILD ACCURACY AND FLUENCY (Reminder)

For all rows and columns, follow the specific directions, then build accuracy and fluency with whole words.

GENERALIZATION (Reminder)

The generalization task provides an opportunity for you to informally assess students' ability to read new words that have not been pretaught.

COMPREHENSION PROCESSES

Understand, Apply

PROCEDURES

1. Introducing the Storybook and Theme

Making Connections; Viewing; Identifying—What, Title, Genre

Have students identify the title of their new story.
Say something like:
Our next two storybooks are about inspiring people.
Inspiring people are people who have done wonderful things.
They make us want to be great too.
Lance Armstrong is a famous bicycle racer.
He inspires other bike riders to work hard and ride long distances.

Dr. Seuss is an inspiring person. He wrote wonderful books. He inspires us to be creative and have fun.

Martin Luther King is an inspiring person. What did he do?
(He worked hard to make life better and fair for all people. He helped make new laws so all people could sit anywhere they wanted on a bus . . .)

THINK ALOUD WITH YOUR STUDENTS

Say something like:
When we say someone is *inspiring*, it means they make us feel good or give us ideas. I wonder how this story will inspire us. What do you think?

TABLE OF CONTENTS

UNIT 21 • A Great Man

2 3

Everyone, look at the cover of the book.
What's the title of this book? (A Great Man)
This book is a nonfiction book. What do you know about it?
(It's a true story.)
The story you will read is about a real person's life. This type of story is called a biography.
What type of story is it? (a biography)

2. Working With the Table of Contents

Using the Table of Contents; Identifying—Titles, Author, Illustrator

- Have students look at the Table of Contents. Say something like:
  How many stories are in the book? (two)
  What's the name of the first story?
  (The 16th President)
  What's the name of the first chapter?
  (Simple Beginnings)
  What page does it begin on? (12)
- Discuss the title page. Say something like:
  Everyone, turn to page 4.

  Who is the author of our new story?
  (Tobi K. Piatek)
  Who is the illustrator? (Larry Johnson)
- Read and discuss the gray text questions.

❶ **Apply:** Viewing; Inferring—Setting; Using Vocabulary—pioneers (It took place a long time ago. It took place during the 1800s, when the pioneers settled the United States . . .)

❷ **Apply:** Inferring; **Understand:** Explaining (There is a log cabin. The man is wearing old-fashioned clothes . . .)

COMPREHENSION PROCESSES

Understand, Apply, Evaluate

PROCEDURES

Introducing Vocabulary

★ **impressive, ordinary**
★ **inspire** ★ **inspiring**
★ **slave** ★ **slavery**

- For each vocabulary word, have students read the word by parts, then read the whole word.
- Read the student-friendly explanations to students as they follow with their fingers. Then have students use the vocabulary word by following the gray text.
- Review and discuss the photos.

USING VOCABULARY

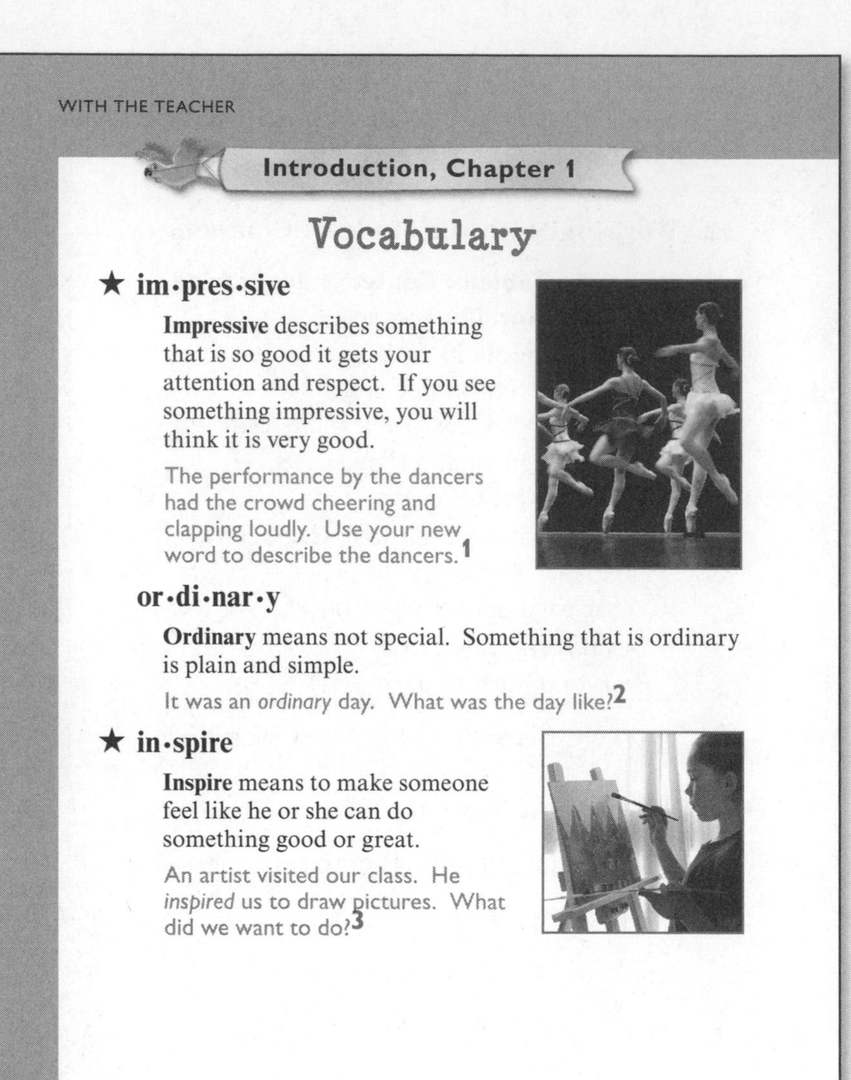

WITH THE TEACHER

Introduction, Chapter 1

Vocabulary

★ **im•pres•sive**

Impressive describes something that is so good it gets your attention and respect. If you see something impressive, you will think it is very good.

The performance by the dancers had the crowd cheering and clapping loudly. Use your new word to describe the dancers.[1]

or•di•nar•y

Ordinary means not special. Something that is ordinary is plain and simple.

It was an *ordinary* day. What was the day like?[2]

★ **in•spire**

Inspire means to make someone feel like he or she can do something good or great.

An artist visited our class. He *inspired* us to draw pictures. What did we want to do?[3]

★ = New

6

❶ **Apply:** Using Vocabulary—impressive (The dancers were impressive.)
❷ **Understand:** Using Vocabulary—ordinary (The day was nothing special.)
❸ **Understand:** Using Vocabulary—inspire (We wanted to draw pictures.)

★ = New in this unit

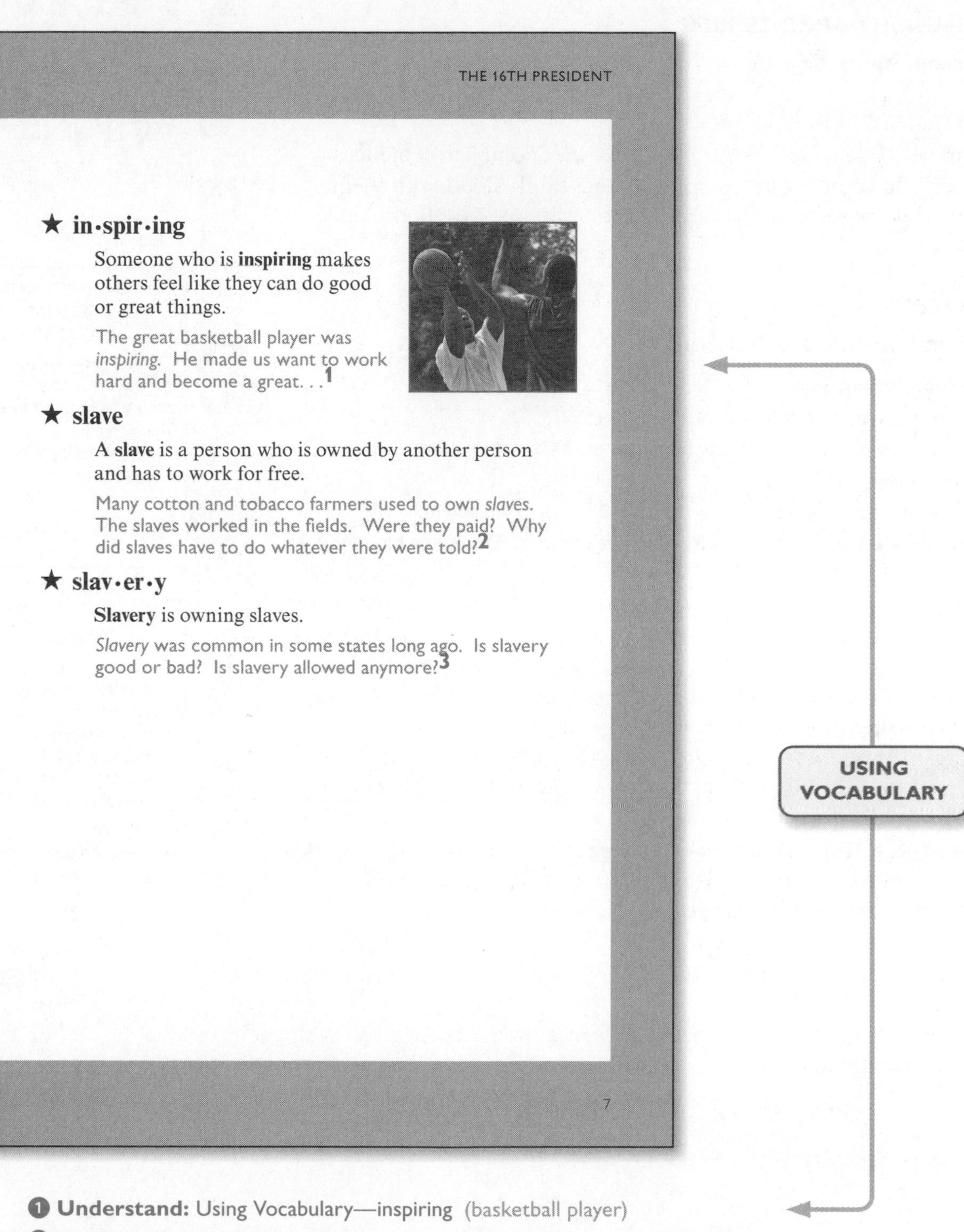

THE 16TH PRESIDENT

★ **in·spir·ing**

Someone who is **inspiring** makes others feel like they can do good or great things.

The great basketball player was *inspiring*. He made us want to work hard and become a great. . .[1]

★ **slave**

A **slave** is a person who is owned by another person and has to work for free.

Many cotton and tobacco farmers used to own *slaves*. The slaves worked in the fields. Were they paid? Why did slaves have to do whatever they were told?[2]

★ **slav·er·y**

Slavery is owning slaves.

Slavery was common in some states long ago. Is slavery good or bad? Is slavery allowed anymore?[3]

7

USING VOCABULARY

❶ **Understand:** Using Vocabulary—inspiring (basketball player)

❷ **Apply:** Inferring; Using Vocabulary—slave (They were not paid. Slaves had to do whatever they were told because they were owned by someone.)

❸ **Evaluate:** Making Judgments; **Apply:** Inferring; Using Vocabulary—slavery, allow (Slavery is bad, so it is not allowed anymore.)

STORY READING INSTRUCTIONS

Students read the Introduction with the teacher and Chapter 1 on their own.

COMPREHENSION PROCESSES

Understand, Apply, Create

COMPREHENSION BUILDING

- Encourage students to answer questions with complete sentences.
- If students have difficulty comprehending, think aloud with them or reread the portion of the story that answers the question. Repeat the question.

CORRECTING DECODING ERRORS

During story reading, gently correct any error, then have students reread the sentence.

PROCEDURES

1. Introducing the Introduction

Viewing, Explaining

Discuss the picture. Say something like:

Turn to page 8 and 9. Look at the pictures. What do you see?

(money, a penny, a statue . . .)

We're going to read about a person who was very inspiring.

If you know who that person is, touch your nose. Don't say his name yet.

REPEATED READINGS

Prosody

On the second reading, students practice developing prosody—phrasing and expression. Research has shown that prosody is related to both fluency and comprehension.

2. First Reading

- Ask questions and discuss the story as indicated by the gray text.
- Mix group and individual turns, independent of your voice. Have students work toward a group accuracy goal of 0–3 errors. Quietly keep track of errors made by all students in the group.
- After reading the story, practice any difficult words. Reread the story if students have not reached the accuracy goal.

3. Second Reading, Short Passage Practice: Developing Prosody

- Demonstrate expressive, fluent reading of the first paragraph. Read at a rate slightly faster than the students' rate.
- Guide practice with your voice.
- Provide individual turns while others track with their fingers and whisper read.
- Repeat with one to three paragraphs at a time. Repeat steps with each remaining paragraph.

Introduction

Look at a shiny U.S. penny. Whose face do you see on it? Look at a five-dollar bill. Who do you see? Both show the picture of a great man. He died about 150 years ago, but the people of the United States still celebrate his birthday every February.

Look at the faces on the penny and five-dollar bill. Do you know who he is?[1]

FINGER TRACKING (Reminder)

To help students keep their places and follow along when others read, continue having them track text with their fingers. Provide positive feedback and individual turns to students who are finger tracking. Say something like: You get a turn because you are following along.

COMPREHENDING AS YOU GO

1 **Apply:** Inferring—Who (He is Abraham Lincoln . . .)

Look at the back of the penny. You can see a picture of the building built in his honor. An impressive marble statue of this great man sits inside the building. The gentle face on the statue looks out across the nation's capital as though he is watching over us all. Can you guess who he is?

How can you tell this person is important?[1]

9

COMPREHENDING AS YOU GO

❶ **Apply:** Inferring, Explaining (They made a memorial of him so people would remember him.)

WITH THE TEACHER

His name is Abraham Lincoln. He was the 16th president of the United States. He led the United States through a very bad time. Lincoln is remembered by people all over the world. He is a very important man in history, but you may be surprised by the story of his life.

Abraham Lincoln, 16th President of the United States

Who is the important person on the U.S. penny and five-dollar bill?[1]
Who was Abraham Lincoln?[2]

10

Priming Background Knowledge

After reading the page, have students explain what they know about Abe Lincoln. Think aloud with students. Say something like: Abe Lincoln is one of my favorite presidents. He inspires me because he was very kind. I wish he were still alive today.

COMPREHENDING AS YOU GO

❶ **Understand:** Identifying—Who (Abraham Lincoln)

❷ **Understand:** Explaining (Abraham Lincoln was the 16th president of the United States.)

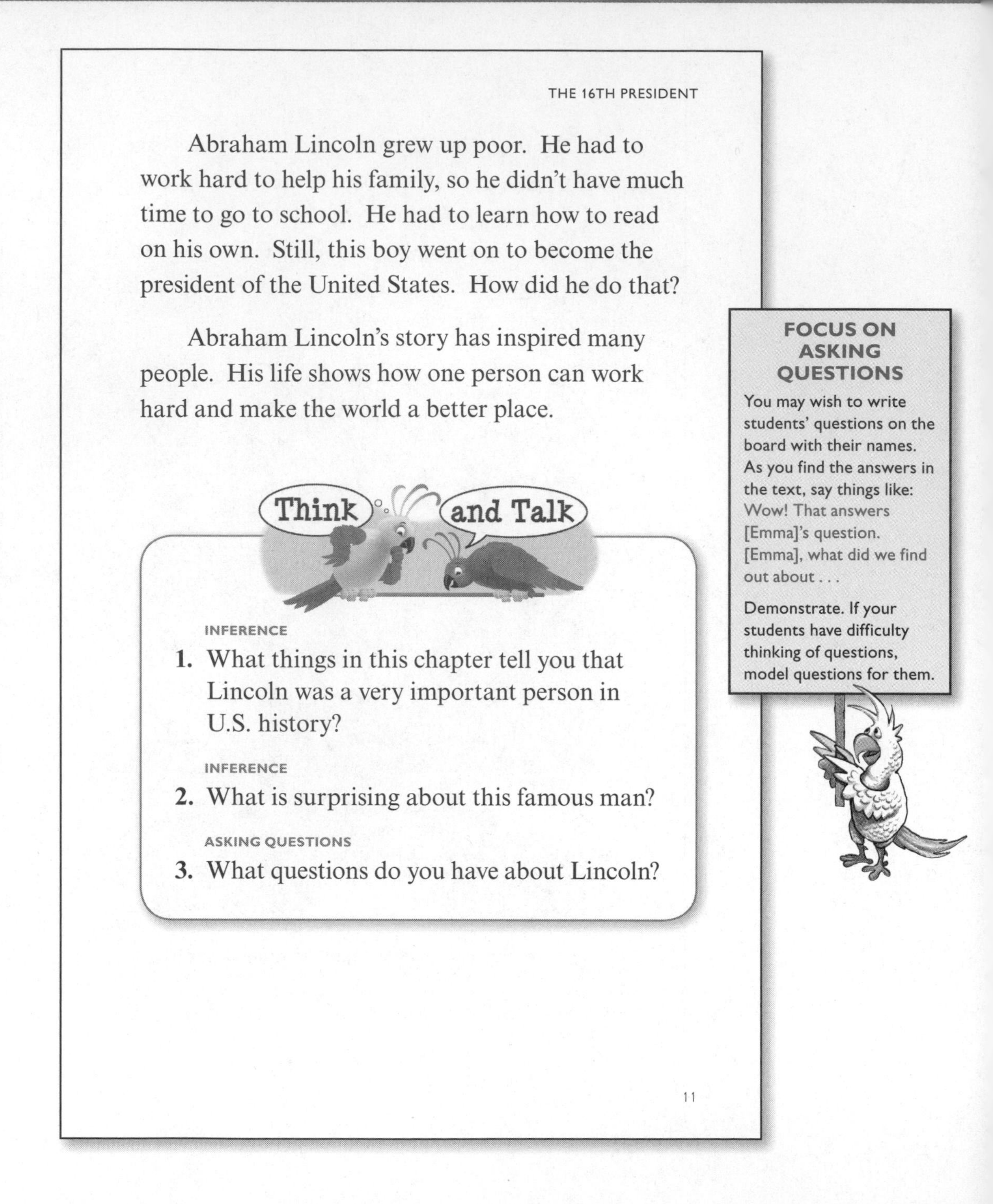

Abraham Lincoln grew up poor. He had to work hard to help his family, so he didn't have much time to go to school. He had to learn how to read on his own. Still, this boy went on to become the president of the United States. How did he do that?

Abraham Lincoln's story has inspired many people. His life shows how one person can work hard and make the world a better place.

INFERENCE

1. What things in this chapter tell you that Lincoln was a very important person in U.S. history?

INFERENCE

2. What is surprising about this famous man?

ASKING QUESTIONS

3. What questions do you have about Lincoln?

FOCUS ON ASKING QUESTIONS

You may wish to write students' questions on the board with their names. As you find the answers in the text, say things like: Wow! That answers [Emma]'s question. [Emma], what did we find out about . . .

Demonstrate. If your students have difficulty thinking of questions, model questions for them.

❶ **Apply:** Inferring, Explaining; Using Vocabulary—memorial (Abraham Lincoln's face is on the penny and the five-dollar bill. There is a memorial of him. He led the country through a very bad time.)

❷ **Apply:** Inferring, Explaining (He grew up poor, and he taught himself to read.)

❸ **Create:** Generating Ideas, Asking Questions (How did he become president? What are some things he did as president . . .)

CHAPTER 1 INSTRUCTIONS

Students read Chapter 1 without the teacher, independently or with partners.

COMPREHENSION PROCESSES

Understand, Apply, Analyze

PROCEDURES FOR READING ON YOUR OWN

1. Getting Ready

Have students turn to page 12.

2. Setting a Purpose

Explaining, Inferring

Before students begin reading, say something like:

On your own, read to find out about Lincoln's early life.

Think about these questions as you read:

- Why did the family move?
- How did Abraham's father feel about slavery?
- What made Abraham's life good?
- What made Abraham's family life hard?

> **PREP NOTE**
> **Setting a Purpose**
> Write questions on a chalkboard, white board, or large piece of paper before working with your small group.

3. Reading on Your Own: Partner or Whisper Reading

- Have students take turns reading every other page with a partner or have students whisper read Chapter 1 on their own.
- Continue having students track each word with their fingers.
- Have students ask themselves or their partners the gray text questions.

For Whisper Reading, say something like:

Everyone, turn to page 12. This is where you're going to start reading on your own—without me. You will whisper read as you track with your finger, so I can see where you are in your work.

Turn to page 14. That's where you are going to stop reading.

Now turn back to page 12.

For Partner Reading, say something like:

Everyone, turn to page 12. This is where you're going to start Partner Reading.

Where are you going to sit? (at our desks, side by side)

You will take turns reading pages. If you are the listener, what will you do? (keep my book flat, follow with my finger, compliment my partner)

If you are the reader, what will you do? (keep my book flat, finger track, read quietly)

Turn to page 14. That's where you are going to stop reading.

4. Comprehension and Skill Work

For students on a 6-Day Plan, tell them they will do Comprehension and Skill Activity 1 and start their Lincoln Mini-Book after they read on their own. Guide practice, as needed. For teacher directions, see pages 27–29. (For 8-Day Plans, see the Lesson Planner, page 9.)

When you finish reading, you'll work on your Comp and Skill Activity 1 and your Lincoln Mini-Book. Your Lincoln Mini-Book is a place for taking notes on Abe Lincoln. Your notes will help you write your own report on Abe Lincoln. You are getting so smart! I am very proud of you.

5. Homework 1: Repeated Reading

Chapter 1

Simple Beginnings

Abraham Lincoln was born in Kentucky on a cold February day in 1809. Abraham, his parents, and his sister, Sarah, lived in a tiny one-room log cabin with a dirt floor. The furniture was made by hand. The mattresses were filled with cornhusks and had bearskin covers. A fire crackling in the fireplace warmed and lit the cabin. The family cooked their meals in a big pot over that fire.

The Kentucky cabin where Lincoln lived as a young boy

Abraham's father, Thomas Lincoln, could not read or write, but the family listened and laughed at his stories and tall tales. Abraham's mother, Nancy Hanks Lincoln, would also read aloud from the Bible. Abraham loved to listen to his parents' stories.

Why do you think Abraham's family told stories? 1

COMPREHENDING AS YOU GO

1 **Analyze:** Drawing Conclusions (They were poor. Back then, no one had a TV or video games . . .)

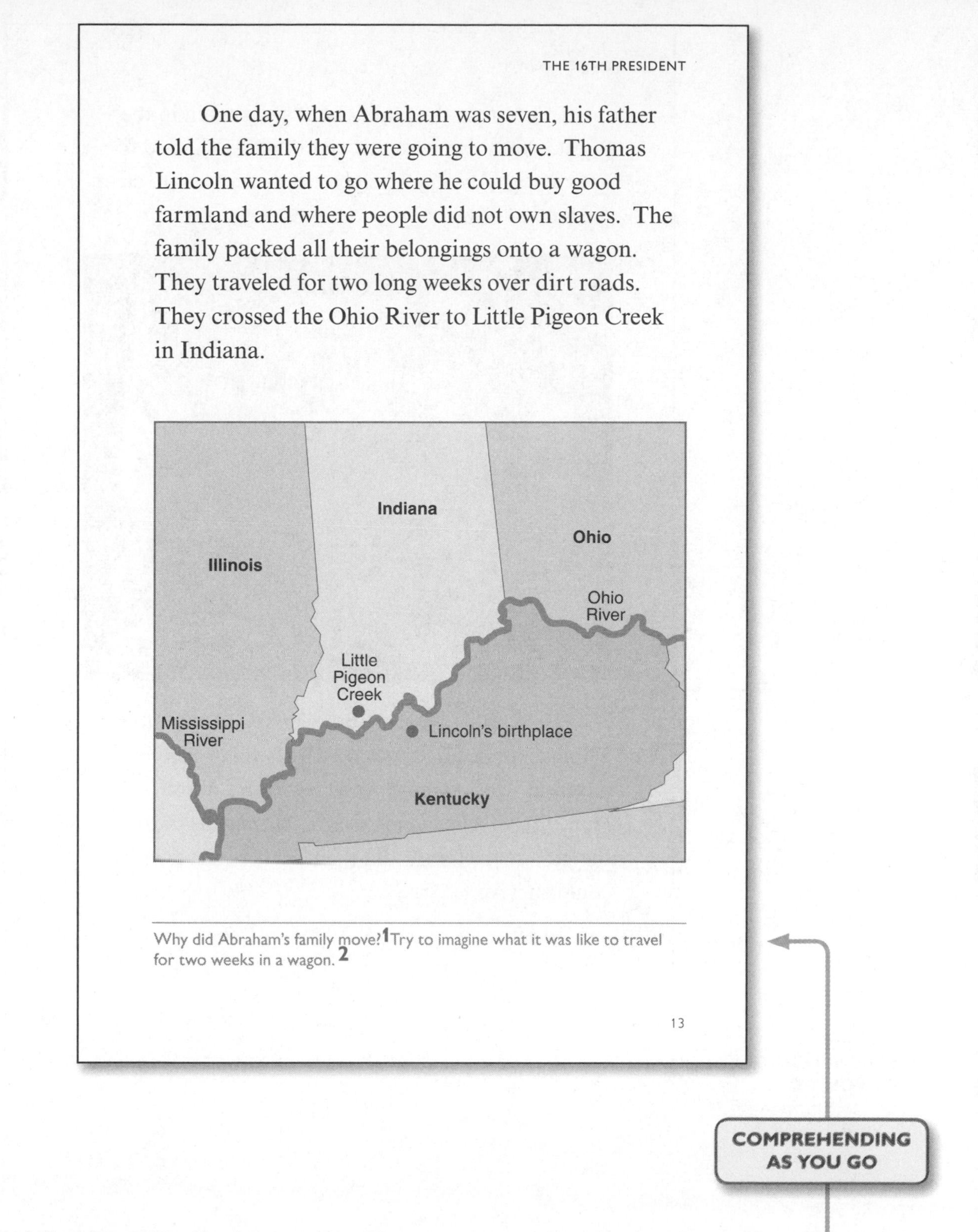

One day, when Abraham was seven, his father told the family they were going to move. Thomas Lincoln wanted to go where he could buy good farmland and where people did not own slaves. The family packed all their belongings onto a wagon. They traveled for two long weeks over dirt roads. They crossed the Ohio River to Little Pigeon Creek in Indiana.

Why did Abraham's family move?[1] Try to imagine what it was like to travel for two weeks in a wagon.[2]

COMPREHENDING AS YOU GO

❶ **Understand:** Explaining: Using Vocabulary—slave (They wanted to go where they could buy good farmland and where people did not own slaves.)

❷ **Understand:** Visualizing

ON YOUR OWN

In Indiana, the family built a log cabin in the forest. Abraham was only eight, but he learned to use an axe. Abraham helped cut down trees to clear the land.

The family worried about having enough to eat. Thomas hunted and fished. The family gathered nuts and fruits from the land near their home. Honey from a beehive was a sweet treat. Abe and the rest of the family did their parts so the family could survive.

What did the family do to survive? 1

14

COMPREHENDING AS YOU GO

1 **Understand:** Explaining; Using Vocabulary—**survive** (The family hunted and fished. They gathered nuts and fruits from the land to survive.)

STORY COMPREHENSION

COMPREHENSION PROCESSES

Understand, Apply, Create

WRITING TRAITS

Ideas and Content
Word Choice
Conventions—Complete Sentence, Capital, Question Mark
Presentation

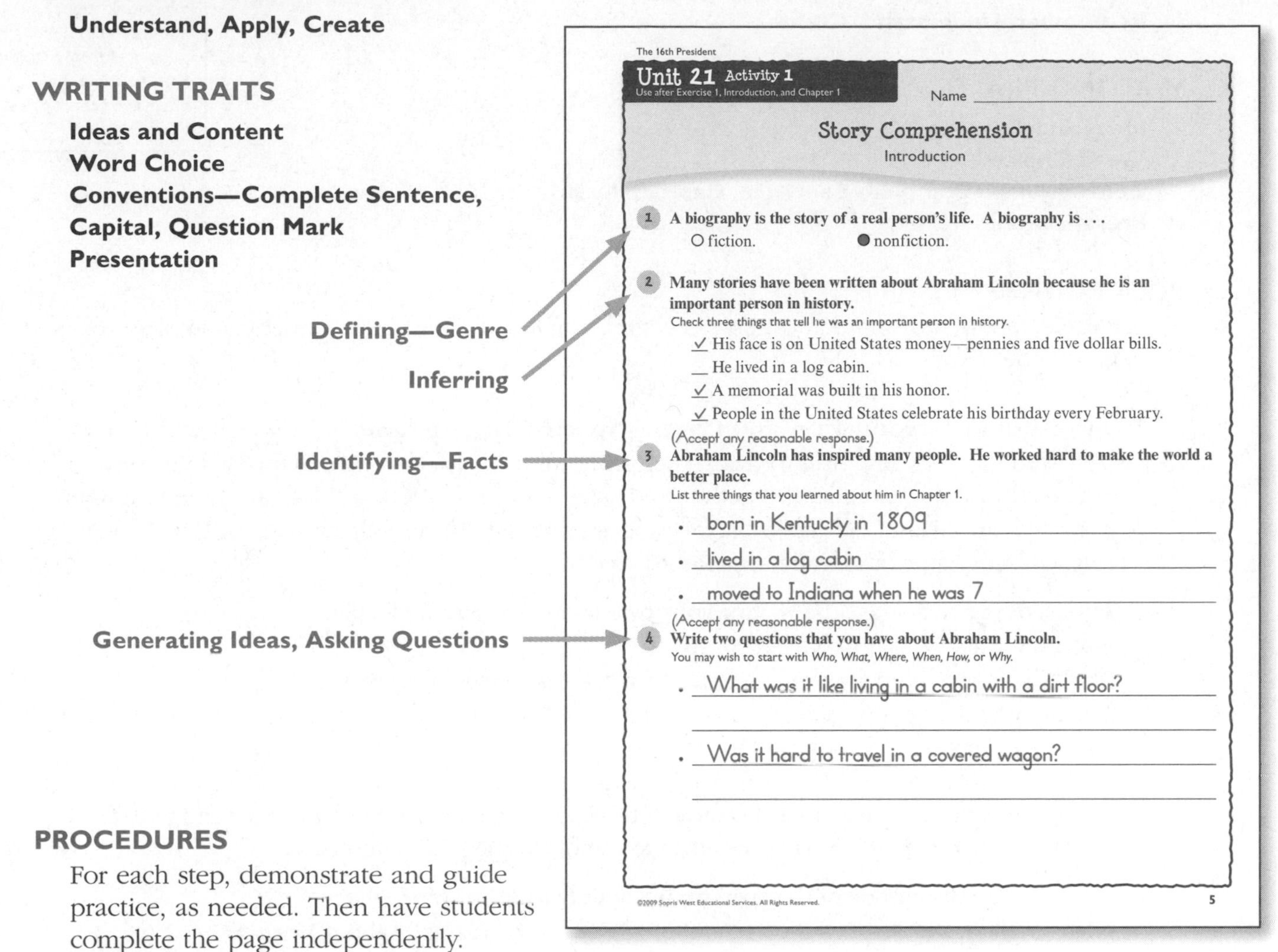

The 16th President

Unit 21 Activity 1
Use after Exercise 1, Introduction, and Chapter 1

Name ____________

Story Comprehension
Introduction

1. **A biography is the story of a real person's life. A biography is . . .**
   ○ fiction. ● nonfiction.

2. **Many stories have been written about Abraham Lincoln because he is an important person in history.**
   Check three things that tell he was an important person in history.
   ✓ His face is on United States money—pennies and five dollar bills.
   __ He lived in a log cabin.
   ✓ A memorial was built in his honor.
   ✓ People in the United States celebrate his birthday every February.

(Accept any reasonable response.)

3. **Abraham Lincoln has inspired many people. He worked hard to make the world a better place.**
   List three things that you learned about him in Chapter 1.
   - born in Kentucky in 1809
   - lived in a log cabin
   - moved to Indiana when he was 7

(Accept any reasonable response.)

4. **Write two questions that you have about Abraham Lincoln.**
   You may wish to start with *Who, What, Where, When, How,* or *Why.*
   - What was it like living in a cabin with a dirt floor?
   - Was it hard to travel in a covered wagon?

5

PROCEDURES

For each step, demonstrate and guide practice, as needed. Then have students complete the page independently.

1. **Selection Response—Basic Instructions** (Items 1, 2)
   Have students read the sentences, then fill in the bubble or check the blank for the correct answer.

2. **Making Lists: Locating Information—Specific Instructions** (Item 3)
   Have students read the directions, then list three things they learned about Abraham Lincoln. Remind students to look back in Chapter 1.

3. **Asking Questions: Sentence Writing—Specific Instructions** (Item 4)
   Have students read the directions and write two questions they have about Abraham Lincoln. Remind them to start questions with a capital and end with a question mark. Have students brainstorm possible questions. You may wish to say something like:
   Abraham Lincoln is one of the most important presidents in U.S. history. I wonder why he is so famous. So one question I have is "Why is Lincoln so famous?" What do you wonder about Lincoln?

Self-monitoring
Have students check and correct their work.

COVER PAGE AND ENTRY 1

> **SPECIAL NOTE**
> Across this unit, your students will complete a mini-book about Lincoln. For ease of use, pull pages 1–4 from *Activity Book 4*. Staple the pages down the center to create a book.

COMPREHENSION PROCESSES

Remember, Understand, Create

WRITING TRAITS

Ideas and Content
Word Choice
Conventions—Complete Sentence, Capital, Period
Presentation

PROCEDURES

For each step, demonstrate and guide practice, as needed. Then have students complete the page independently.

1. **Mini-Book: Introduction and Cover—Specific Instructions**
   Tell students they're going to make their own mini-book about Abraham Lincoln. Have them fill in their name as the author and begin thinking about a title. Say something like:
   Every country has an interesting history and great leaders. After you learn about Lincoln, you might want to study the leader of another country.

   For now, you're going to be writing your own mini-book about Lincoln.
   Read the title. (Abraham Lincoln: blank)
   You're going to write a word or phrase that describes Lincoln in the blank.
   Lincoln was the 16th president, so we could write "The 16th President" in the blank. What else might you write?
   (Lincoln: Awesome President, Lincoln: Great Man . . .)
   Those would all be great titles. I want you to keep your ideas. After you've read and written more about Lincoln, you will know what you want to title your mini-book.

   Who will be the author of this mini-book about Lincoln? (We will.)
   That's right. Each of you will be an author of your own biography about Lincoln.

2. **Caption Writing—Specific Instructions**
   Have students look at the photo, then write an appropriate caption. Remind them to start their caption with a capital, use a capital for Lincoln's name, and end with a period.

3. **Paragraph Writing—Specific Instructions**
   - Have students write a paragraph summarizing Abraham Lincoln's early life. Remind them to use capitals and periods.
   - Think aloud with students and brainstorm possible answers.

Generating—Title
Identifying—Author

Unit 21 Abraham Lincoln Mini-Book

Abraham Lincoln:
Our 16th President

by Nancy

Unit 21 Abraham Lincoln Mini-Book

Entry 1 Chapter 1

Simple Beginnings

Viewing
Generating Ideas
Sentence Writing

Write a caption for this photo.

Abraham and his family lived in a small log cabin with a dirt floor.

Summarizing—Facts
Sentence Writing

Write at least 2 sentences that tell about Abe Lincoln's early life.

Abraham and his family moved to Indiana when he was seven. They built a log cabin and hunted for their food.

1

❶ SOUND REVIEW

❷ ACCURACY AND FLUENCY BUILDING

B1. Reading by Analogy

Have students figure out how to read *-arry* by reading other words they know.
Use the words in sentences, as needed.

C1. Multisyllabic Words

- For the list of words divided by syllables, have students read each syllable, then the whole word. Use the word in a sentence, as appropriate.
- For the list of whole words, build accuracy and then fluency.

afford The expensive bike was more than Andy could . . . *afford.*
preacher The person who speaks to everyone in church is the . . . *preacher.*
peddlers People who go door to door and sell things are . . . *peddlers.*
imitated The monkey did what the clown did. He . . . *imitated* . . . the clown.
pioneer The first person to live in a new place is called a . . . *pioneer.*
harvest The vegetables were ripe, so it was time for the . . . *harvest.*

ACCURACY AND FLUENCY BUILDING (Reminder)

For each task, have students say any underlined part, then read the word.

Set a pace. Then have students read the whole words in each task and column.

Provide repeated practice, building accuracy first, then fluency.

D1. Tricky Words

- For each Tricky Word, have students use the sounds and word parts they know to silently sound out the word. Use the word in a sentence to help with pronunciation.

encourage
Look at the first word. What is the small word you already know? (courage)
Read the word by parts to yourselves and use my sentence to figure out the word.
The teacher will cheer her students on. She will . . . *encourage* . . . them.
Read the word three times. (encourage, encourage, encourage)

cousin
Look at the next word. The o doesn't do anything in this word. Read the word. (cousin)
My uncle and aunt's child is my . . . *cousin.* Read the word two times. (cousin, cousin)

borrow It's important to return things that you . . . *borrow.*
schooling If you want to learn, you need . . . *schooling.*
fields We had fun picking wildflowers in the . . . *fields.*
hero Someone who saves someone else is a . . . *hero.*

- Have students go back and read the whole words in the column.

❸ WORDS IN CONTEXT

❹ NAMES

❺ MORPHOGRAPHS AND AFFIXES

- Have students read the underlined part, then the whole word.
- Review the morphographs *bi-*, *-ful*, and *-un*, as time allows. Say something like:
  Put your finger on the first word in Row B.
  Read the underlined part, then the word. (bi, bicoastal)
  What does *bi-* mean? (two) Right, so bicoastal means on two . . . coasts.
- Repeat practice, building accuracy, then fluency.

6 GENERALIZATION: READING NEW WORDS IN PARAGRAPHS

- Have students read the paragraph silently, then out loud. Tell students to use the sounds and word parts they know to read any difficult words.
- Repeat practice, as needed.

The 16th President

Unit 21 Exercise 2

Use before Chapters 2 and 3

1. SOUND REVIEW Use selected Sound Cards from Units 1–19.

2. ACCURACY/FLUENCY BUILDING For each column, have students say any underlined part, then read each word. Next, have them read the column.

A1 Mixed Practice	B1 Reading by Analogy	C1 Multisyllabic Words		D1 Tricky Words
plow	carry	af•ford	afford	encourage
key	Larry	preach•er	preacher	cousin
fences	marry	ped•dlers	peddlers	borrow
widow	remarry	im•i•tat•ed	imitated	schooling
laws	remarried	pi•o•neer	pioneer	fields
copy		har•vest	harvest	hero

3. WORDS IN CONTEXT Have students use the sounds and word parts they know to figure out each word. Then have them read each sentence.

A	con•gre•ga•tion	A congregation is the group of people who go to a church.
B	kind-heart•ed	A kind-hearted girl rescued the wet kitten from the rain.

4. NAMES Have students use the sounds and word parts they know to figure out the words.

George Washington	Sarah Bush Johnston	the Lincolns

5. MORPHOGRAPHS AND AFFIXES Have students read each underlined part, then the word.

A	attention	government	important	buildable
B	bicoastal	watchful	unused	regularity

6. GENERALIZATION Have students read the paragraph silently, then out loud. (New words: speech, speakers)

I decided to run for class president, so I had to give a speech in class. I was the first of three speakers. I was nervous but ready to do my best. I spoke in a clear voice. When I was done, everyone clapped. I was proud of myself.

2

KEEP LESSONS MOVING WITH FINGER TRACKING (Reminder)

Always require finger tracking. This will:
- Prevent having to stop to help students find their places.
- Ensure students are practicing even when it's someone else's turn.
- Allow you to monitor on-task behavior.
- Increase focus and accuracy.

COMPREHENSION PROCESSES

Understand, Apply

PROCEDURES

1. Introducing Vocabulary

widow ★encourage, pioneer ★imitate ★government ★expensive

- For each vocabulary word, have students read the word by parts, then read the whole word.
- Read the student-friendly explanations to students as they follow with their fingers. Then have students use the vocabulary word by following the gray text.
- Review and discuss the photos and illustrations.

USING VOCABULARY

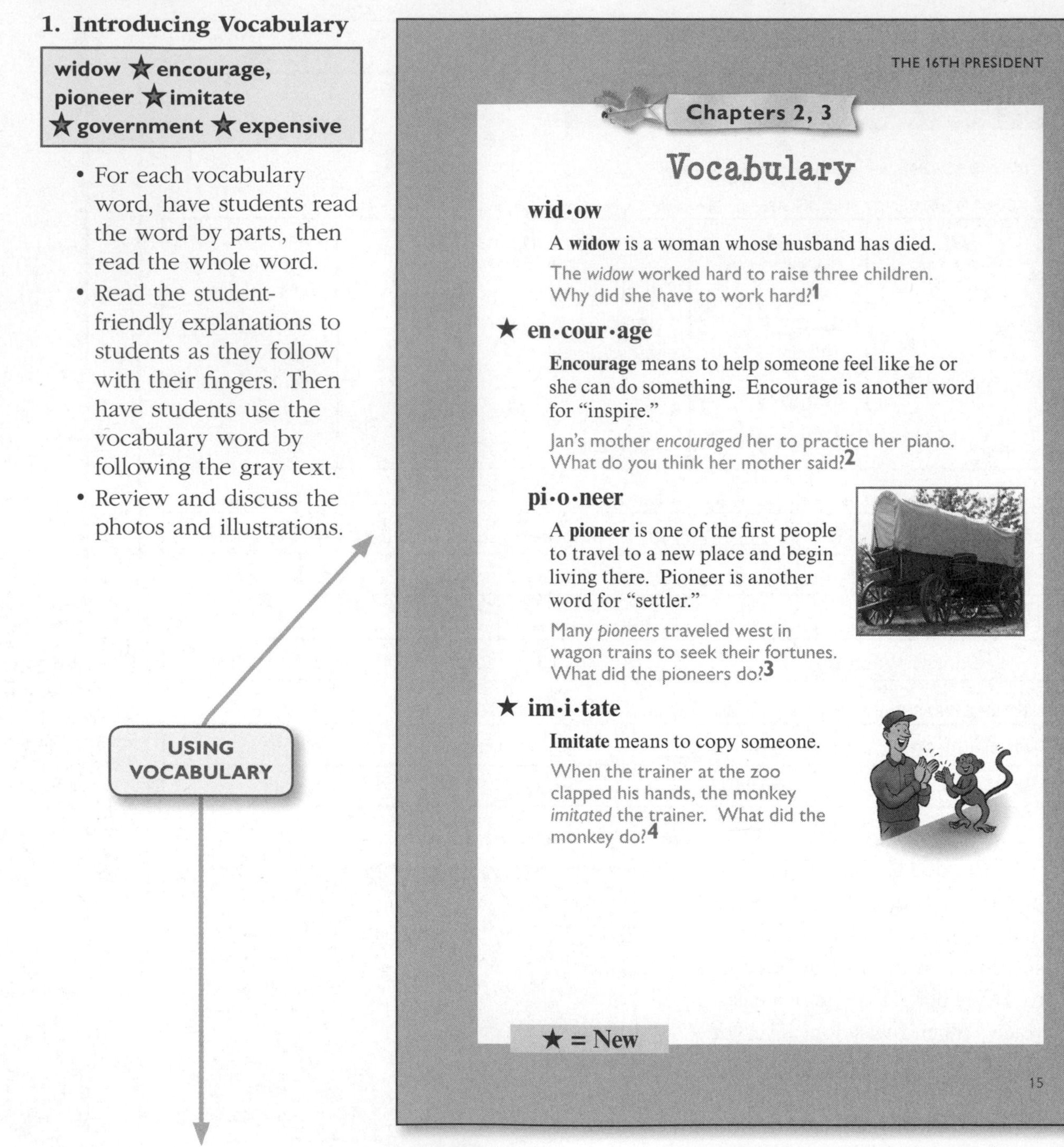

THE 16TH PRESIDENT

Chapters 2, 3

Vocabulary

wid•ow

A **widow** is a woman whose husband has died.

The *widow* worked hard to raise three children. Why did she have to work hard?[1]

★ **en•cour•age**

Encourage means to help someone feel like he or she can do something. Encourage is another word for "inspire."

Jan's mother *encouraged* her to practice her piano. What do you think her mother said?[2]

pi•o•neer

A **pioneer** is one of the first people to travel to a new place and begin living there. Pioneer is another word for "settler."

Many *pioneers* traveled west in wagon trains to seek their fortunes. What did the pioneers do?[3]

★ **im•i•tate**

Imitate means to copy someone.

When the trainer at the zoo clapped his hands, the monkey *imitated* the trainer. What did the monkey do?[4]

★ = New

15

❶ **Apply:** Inferring; Using Vocabulary—widow (The widow had to work hard to raise three children because her husband died and she was on her own. She had to make sure the children had enough to eat and a home . . .)

❷ **Apply:** Using Vocabulary—encourage (Jan, I love hearing you play the piano. You are becoming a great musician . . .)

❸ **Understand:** Using Vocabulary—pioneer (The pioneers traveled west.)

❹ **Understand:** Using Vocabulary—imitate (The monkey copied the trainer.)

★ = New in this unit

2. Now You Try It!

- Read or paraphrase the directions.
- Have students read the word by parts, then read the whole word.
- Have students explain or define the word in their own words. Say something like:
  Look at the word. Say the parts, then read the whole word.
  (ex•pen•sive, expensive)
  Now, let's pretend that we're going to explain or define the word *expensive* to a friend. [Caitlin], what would you say?
  Start with "Something is expensive when . . . "
  (Something is expensive when it costs a lot.)
  That's right. Something is expensive when it costs a lot of money.
- Have students turn to the appropriate page in the glossary and discuss how their definition is the same or different than the glossary's. Your students may like their definition better.

Note: By defining a word in their own words, students are demonstrating depth of word knowledge. Verbatim responses only demonstrate memorization. Encourage paraphrasing.

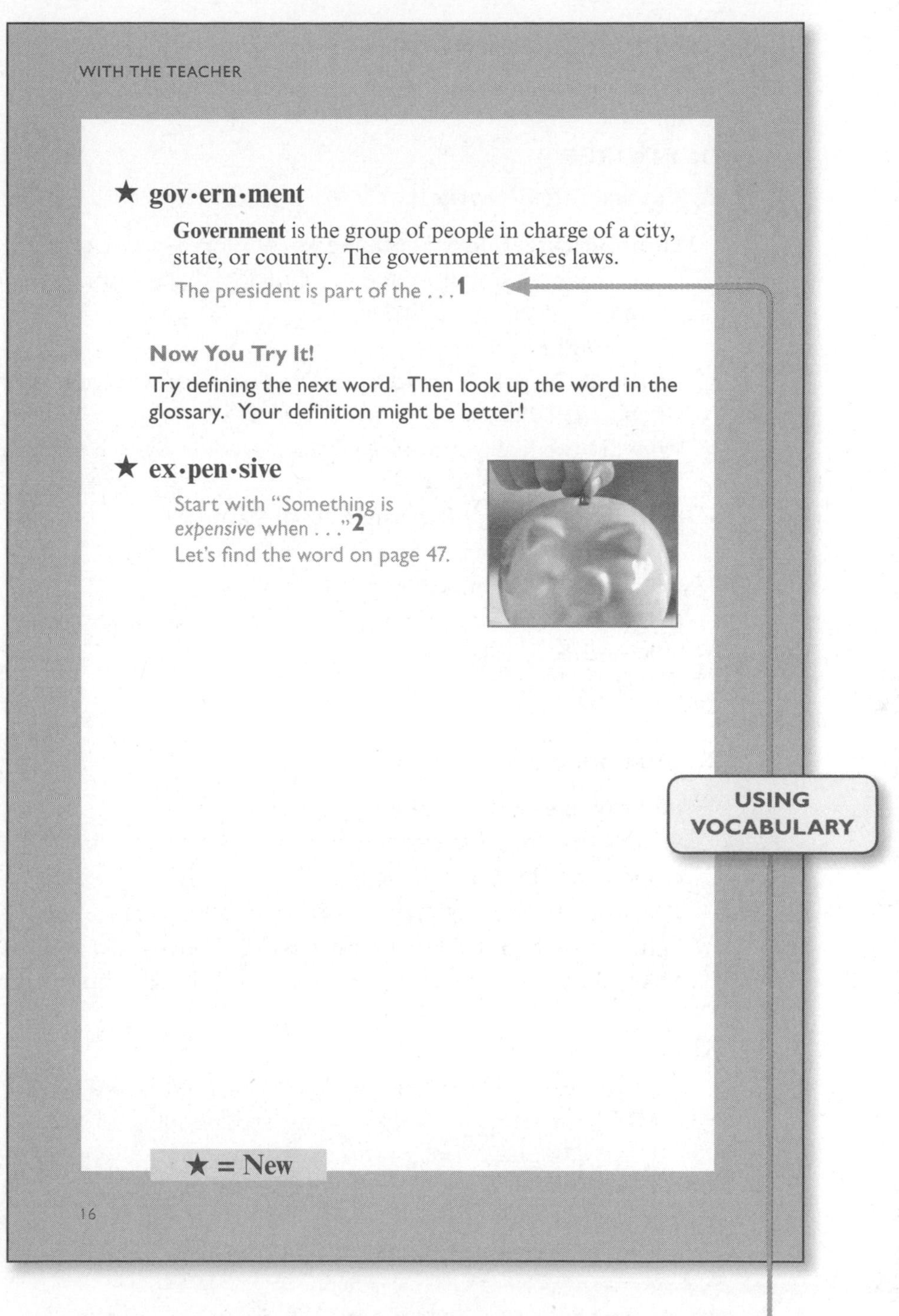

❶ **Apply:** Using Vocabulary—government (government)

❷ **Understand:** Defining and Using Vocabulary—expensive; Using Glossary (Something is expensive when it costs a lot of money.)

CHAPTER 2 INSTRUCTIONS

Students read Chapter 2 with the teacher and Chapter 3 on their own.
Note: If you're working on an 8-Day Plan, you will read Chapter 3 with students.

COMPREHENSION PROCESSES

Remember, Understand, Apply, Analyze, Create

PROCEDURES

1. Reviewing Chapter 1

Summarizing; Inferring; Using Vocabulary—slave, slavery

Have students turn to page 12. Quickly discuss the questions from Chapter 1, Setting a Purpose.

Say something like:

You read Chapter 1 on your own. Let's review what you learned about Lincoln's childhood.

Why did the family move? (Abraham's father wanted to move to a place where he could buy good farmland and people did not own slaves . . .)

How did Abraham's father feel about slavery?
(He didn't like it. He wanted to move away from it.)

What made Abraham's life good?
(His family worked together. They told stories and laughed.)

What made Abraham's family life hard?
(The family was very poor. They worried about having enough food.)

2. Introducing Chapter 2

Identifying—Title; Defining—Genre

What's the title of this chapter? (Young Abraham)

Remember, this is a biography.

What makes this story a biography? (It tells about someone's life.)

In this chapter, you'll learn what Abraham Lincoln did as a young boy.

Think about what helped make this ordinary young boy a great man.

3. First Reading

- Ask questions and discuss the story as indicated by the gray text.
- Mix group and individual turns, independent of your voice.
  Have students work toward a group accuracy goal of 0–4 errors.
  Quietly keep track of errors made by all students in the group.
- After reading the story, practice any difficult words.
  Reread the story if students have not reached the accuracy goal.

4. Second Reading, Timed Readings: Repeated Reading

- As time allows, have students do Timed Readings while others follow along.
- Time individuals for 30 seconds and encourage each child to work for a personal best.
- Determine words correct per minute. Record student scores.

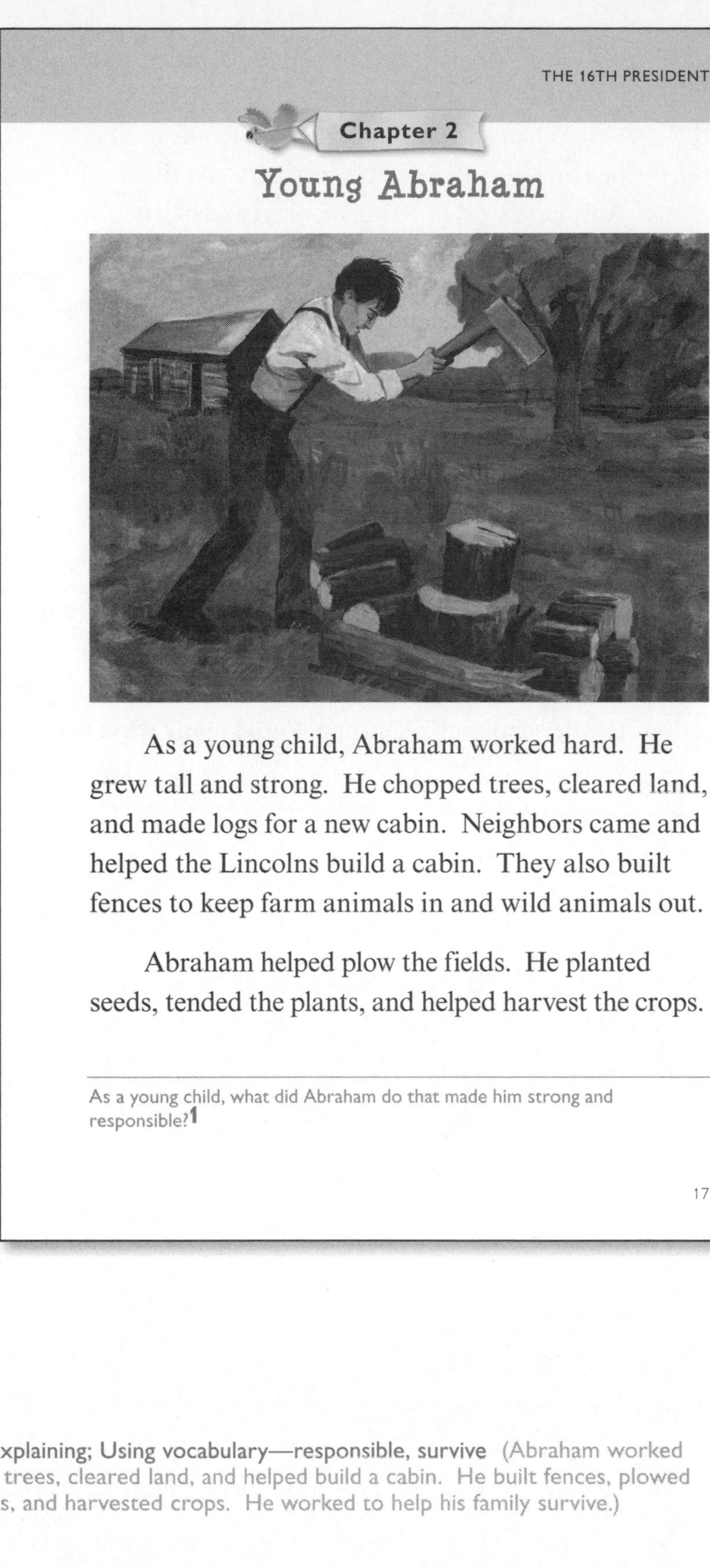

THE 16TH PRESIDENT

Chapter 2

Young Abraham

As a young child, Abraham worked hard. He grew tall and strong. He chopped trees, cleared land, and made logs for a new cabin. Neighbors came and helped the Lincolns build a cabin. They also built fences to keep farm animals in and wild animals out.

Abraham helped plow the fields. He planted seeds, tended the plants, and helped harvest the crops.

As a young child, what did Abraham do that made him strong and responsible?1

17

FOCUS ON CONTRASTING

Visualizing

After completing the page, say something like:
Close your eyes and imagine getting up in the morning. There is no heat. It's cold, but the air is fresh.

Now, imagine going outside. You are not on your way to school. You can't go. There is too much work to be done.

You lift up an axe and begin chopping wood. The sun is hot, and your skin gets sticky from the hard work, but your mother is proud of you.

You stop for lunch. You are very tired, but your mother, father, and sister all gather and tell stories. There are fresh berries for lunch and a small amount of soup and bread.

There isn't much to eat. Soon it is time to go back to work. You help your father pull brush, cut logs, and haul them back to the cabin. The sun is hot, and the work is hard, but your father is very proud of you.

Open your eyes. Now that you've imagined Abe's life, what was it like? How was it different from yours?

COMPREHENDING AS YOU GO

❶ **Apply:** Inferring, Explaining; Using vocabulary—responsible, survive (Abraham worked hard. He chopped trees, cleared land, and helped build a cabin. He built fences, plowed fields, planted crops, and harvested crops. He worked to help his family survive.)

WITH THE TEACHER

When Abraham was only nine, his mother became ill and died. It was a very sad time. Abraham's sister, Sarah, cooked and cleaned. Abraham and his father worked in the fields.

The Lincolns were a happy family again when their father remarried a kind-hearted widow, Sarah Bush Johnston. Sarah and her three children all moved into the tiny cabin. A cousin lived there too. Even though it was crowded, Abraham's new stepmother made their home a happy place where Abraham was encouraged to read and learn.

Abraham had no library near his home. Books were expensive, and very few people owned more than one or two. Though he had few books and only a little schooling, Abraham found many ways to learn.

What made life hard for Abe and his sister?1 What would you do to learn new things if you didn't have books and couldn't go to school?2

18

COMPREHENDING AS YOU GO

❶ **Understand:** Explaining (Their mother died. There was too much work to be done.)

❷ **Create:** Generating Ideas; **Apply:** Using Vocabulary—experiment (I would ask people questions. I would conduct experiments . . .)

Abraham talked to the people he met. He met pioneers moving west and peddlers carrying things to sell, like cloth, seeds, and shovels. He met traders, preachers, teachers, and farmers. Abraham talked to them—as many as he could—and learned as much as he could.

Who did Abraham learn from?[1]

COMPREHENDING AS YOU GO

1 **Understand:** Explaining; Using Vocabulary—pioneer, trader (Abraham learned from the people he met. He learned from pioneers, peddlers, traders, preachers, teachers, and farmers.)

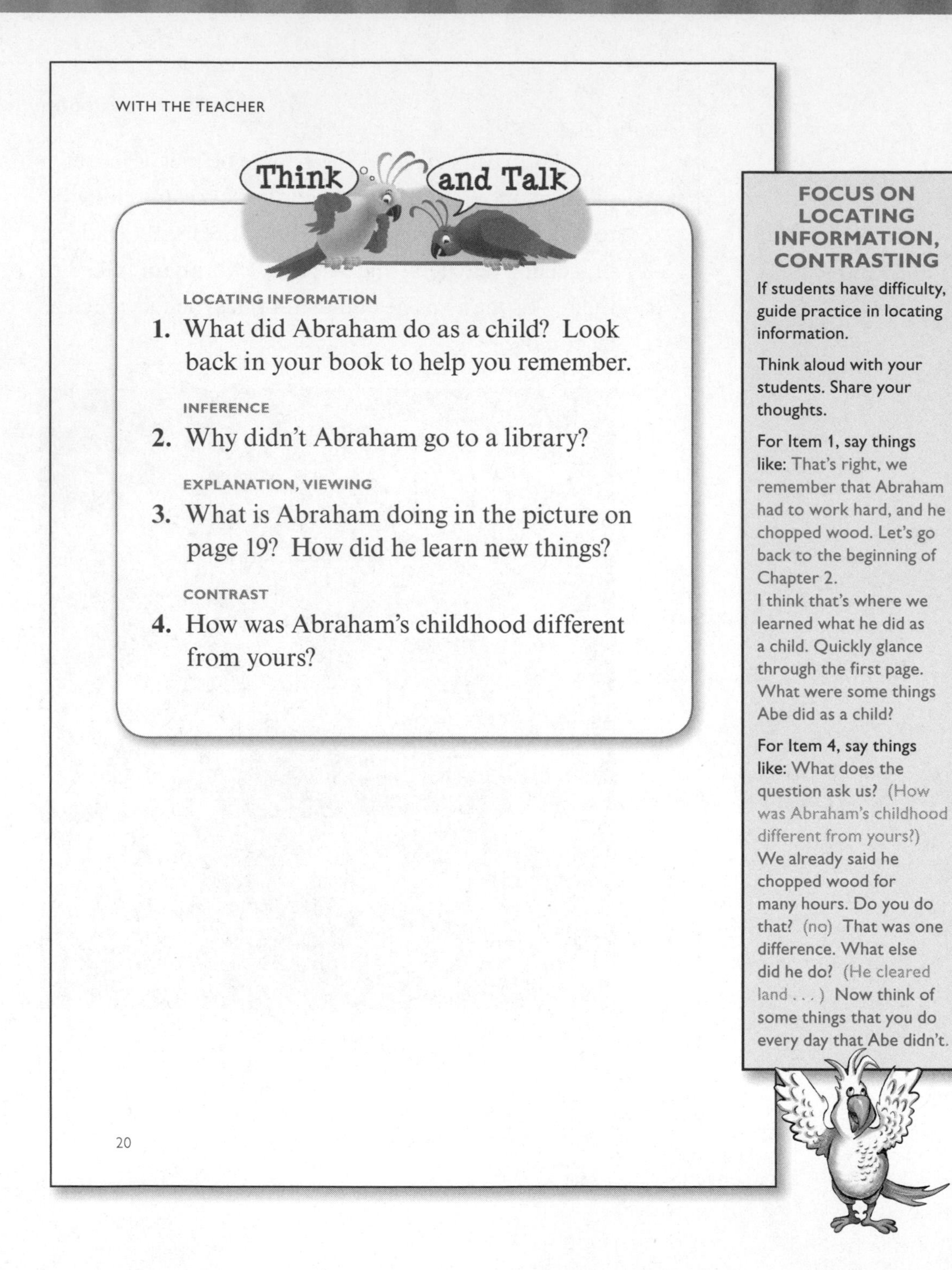

FOCUS ON LOCATING INFORMATION, CONTRASTING

If students have difficulty, guide practice in locating information.

Think aloud with your students. Share your thoughts.

For Item 1, say things like: That's right, we remember that Abraham had to work hard, and he chopped wood. Let's go back to the beginning of Chapter 2. I think that's where we learned what he did as a child. Quickly glance through the first page. What were some things Abe did as a child?

For Item 4, say things like: What does the question ask us? (How was Abraham's childhood different from yours?) We already said he chopped wood for many hours. Do you do that? (no) That was one difference. What else did he do? (He cleared land . . .) Now think of some things that you do every day that Abe didn't.

❶ **Understand:** Explaining, Locating Information (He had to work hard. He chopped trees, built fences, plowed fields, and planted crops. He hunted and fished to help his family get food . . .)

❷ **Apply:** Inferring, Explaining (There was no library near his home.)

❸ **Understand:** Viewing, Explaining (Abraham is talking to a traveler. Talking to the people he met is how he learned things.)

❹ **Analyze:** Contrasting (Abraham didn't have a TV or books, and I have a TV, books, and videos. Abraham had to work hard outside all the time, and I almost never have to work outside . . .)

CHAPTER 3 INSTRUCTIONS

Students read Chapter 3 without the teacher, independently or with partners. *Note*: If you're working on an 8-Day Plan, you will read Chapter 3 with students.

COMPREHENSION PROCESSES

Remember, Understand, Apply, Analyze, Evaluate

PROCEDURES FOR READING ON YOUR OWN

1. Getting Ready

Have students turn to page 21.

2. Setting a Purpose

Explaining; Inferring

Before students begin reading, say something like:

The next chapter tells other ways that Abraham found to learn new things. The questions you should think about as you read are on the board. When you finish Chapter 3, be ready to answers these questions:

- How did Abraham feel about school?
- What does the book say that leads you to think Abraham loved to read?

> **PREP NOTE**
> **Setting a Purpose**
> Write questions on a chalkboard, white board, or large piece of paper before working with your small group.

3. Reading on Your Own: Partner or Whisper Reading

- Have students take turns reading every other page with a partner or have students whisper read on their own.
- Continue having students track each word with their fingers.
- Have students ask themselves or their partners the gray text questions.

4. Comprehension and Skill Work

For students on a 6-Day Plan, tell them they will do Comprehension and Skill Activity 2 and work on their Lincoln Mini-Book after they read on their own. Guide practice, as needed. For teacher directions, see pages 43–44. (For 8-Day Plans, see the Lesson Planner, page 9.)

5. Homework 2: Repeated Reading

ON YOUR OWN

Chapter 3

Abraham Learns

Abraham discovered that he could learn about other places and other people by listening to their stories. But Abraham wanted to know more.

Sometimes in the winter, when the farm work was done, he and Sarah were allowed to go to school. They walked for miles to get there. At school, Abraham learned to read, write, and "reckon" with numbers. Sometimes he found it hard to learn. But once he learned something, he did not forget it.

What did Abraham learn at school?[1] What do you think "reckon" with numbers means?[2]

21

COMPREHENDING AS YOU GO

1. **Remember:** Identifying—What (He learned to read, write, and reckon with numbers.)
2. **Apply:** Inferring, Explaining (It means to count. It means to do math . . .)

ON YOUR OWN

School learning made Abraham hungry to know more. He wanted to know about important ideas and people. He wanted to read about great adventures and discoveries. The boy who would one day become president loved to read about government and presidents! George Washington, the first president of the United States, was his hero.

Abraham read and learned. Books held the key to the things he wanted to learn. But how could he get books? Abraham would walk for miles to borrow a book. He said, "My best friend is a person who will give me a book I have not read."

Who inspired Lincoln to be a leader? 1 Is there anything so important to you that you would walk miles to borrow it? 2

22

COMPREHENDING AS YOU GO

1 **Remember:** Identifying—Who; **Understand:** Using Vocabulary—inspired (George Washington inspired Abraham Lincoln to be a leader.)

2 **Evaluate:** Responding, Making Judgments (No, I don't like to walk far. Yes, I would walk miles for a new Magic Tree House book . . .)

Abraham listened to people talk. In church, he listened to the way that the preacher talked to the congregation. He noticed how the preacher used his voice and his hands to get people's attention. After church, his friends laughed as Abraham stood on a stump and imitated the preacher's words and voice.

Abraham listened to other speakers too. Sometimes people made speeches about slavery. Some people said that everyone should be able to own slaves. Others thought slavery was wrong. Abraham read. He listened, and he learned.

Do you think Abraham agreed with everyone he listened to? [1] How do you think Abraham felt about *slavery*? Why? [2]

COMPREHENDING AS YOU GO

1. **Analyze:** Drawing Conclusions; **Apply:** Using Vocabulary—slave (He probably didn't agree with people who said everyone should be able to own slaves.)
2. **Analyze:** Drawing Conclusions; **Apply:** Using Vocabulary—slavery (I think Abraham felt slavery was wrong because his father thought it was wrong.)

STORY COMPREHENSION • LOCATING INFORMATION

MAZE READING

COMPREHENSION PROCESSES

Understand

WRITING TRAITS

Presentation

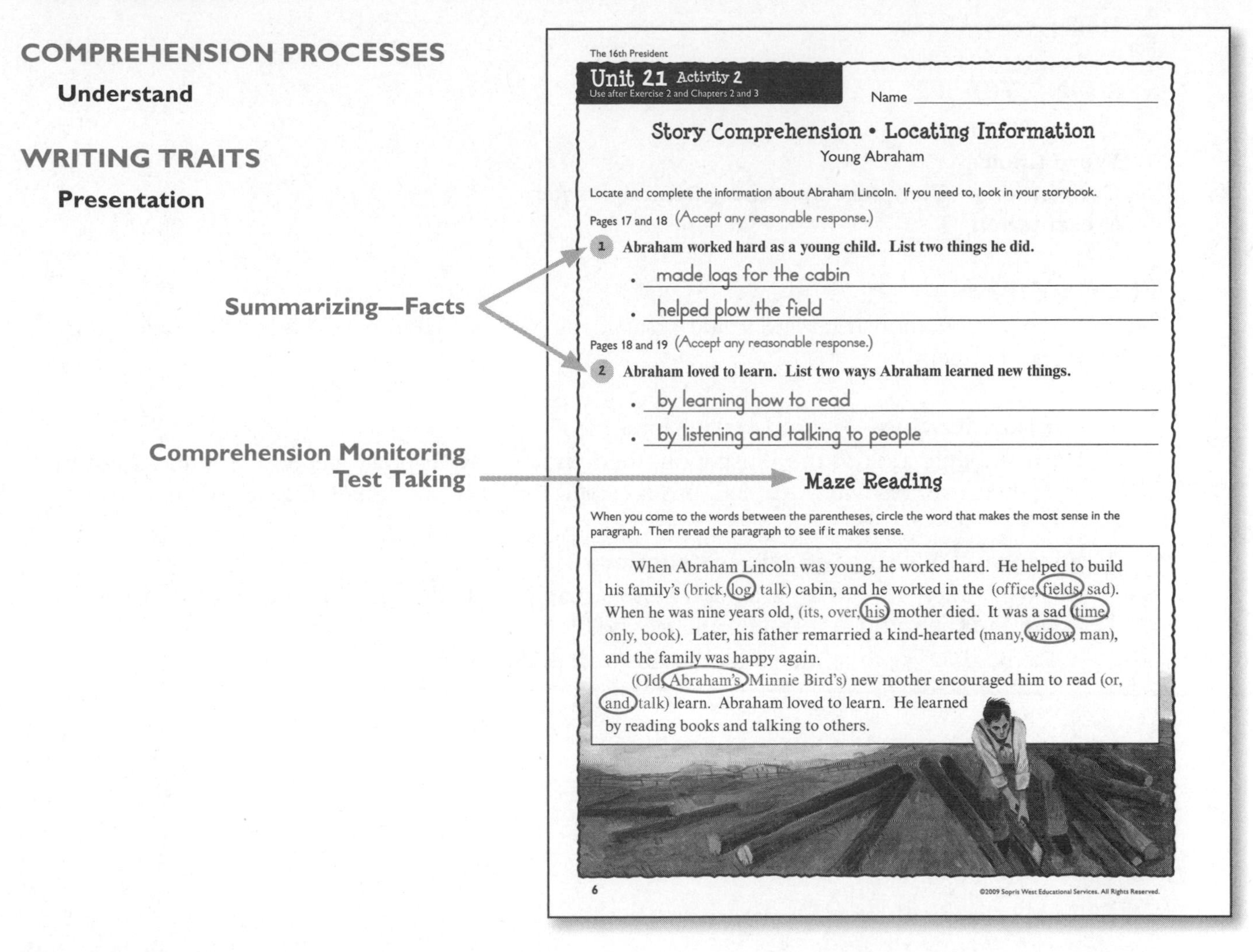

The 16th President

Unit 21 Activity 2
Use after Exercise 2 and Chapters 2 and 3

Name ______________________

Story Comprehension • Locating Information

Young Abraham

Locate and complete the information about Abraham Lincoln. If you need to, look in your storybook.

Pages 17 and 18 (Accept any reasonable response.)

1. **Abraham worked hard as a young child. List two things he did.**
   - made logs for the cabin
   - helped plow the field

Pages 18 and 19 (Accept any reasonable response.)

2. **Abraham loved to learn. List two ways Abraham learned new things.**
   - by learning how to read
   - by listening and talking to people

Maze Reading

When you come to the words between the parentheses, circle the word that makes the most sense in the paragraph. Then reread the paragraph to see if it makes sense.

When Abraham Lincoln was young, he worked hard. He helped to build his family's (brick, log, talk) cabin, and he worked in the (office, fields, sad). When he was nine years old, (its, over, his) mother died. It was a sad (time, only, book). Later, his father remarried a kind-hearted (many, widow, man), and the family was happy again.

(Old, Abraham's, Minnie Bird's) new mother encouraged him to read (or, and, talk) learn. Abraham loved to learn. He learned by reading books and talking to others.

6

PROCEDURES

For each step, demonstrate and guide practice, as needed. Then have students complete the page independently.

Locating Information: Making Lists—Specific Instructions (Items 1, 2)
Have students read the directions for each item, then list two facts. Remind students to look back in their storybooks. Remind them to use a capital if they use Abraham's name.

Maze Reading—Basic Instructions
Have students read the paragraphs and select the word in the parentheses that best completes each sentence.

Self-monitoring
Have students check and correct their work.

ENTRY 2

COMPREHENSION PROCESSES

Understand, Create

WRITING TRAITS

Ideas and Content
Word Choice
Conventions—Complete Sentence, Capital, Period
Presentation

PROCEDURES

For each step, demonstrate and guide practice, as needed. Then have students complete the page independently.

1. **Caption Writing—Basic Instructions**
   Have students look at the illustration, then write an appropriate caption. Remind them to start their caption with a capital, use a capital for Lincoln's name, and end with a period.

2. **Paragraph Writing—Basic Instructions**
   - Have students write a paragraph summarizing Abraham Lincoln's life as a young boy. Remind them to use capitals and periods.
   - Think aloud with students and brainstorm possible answers.

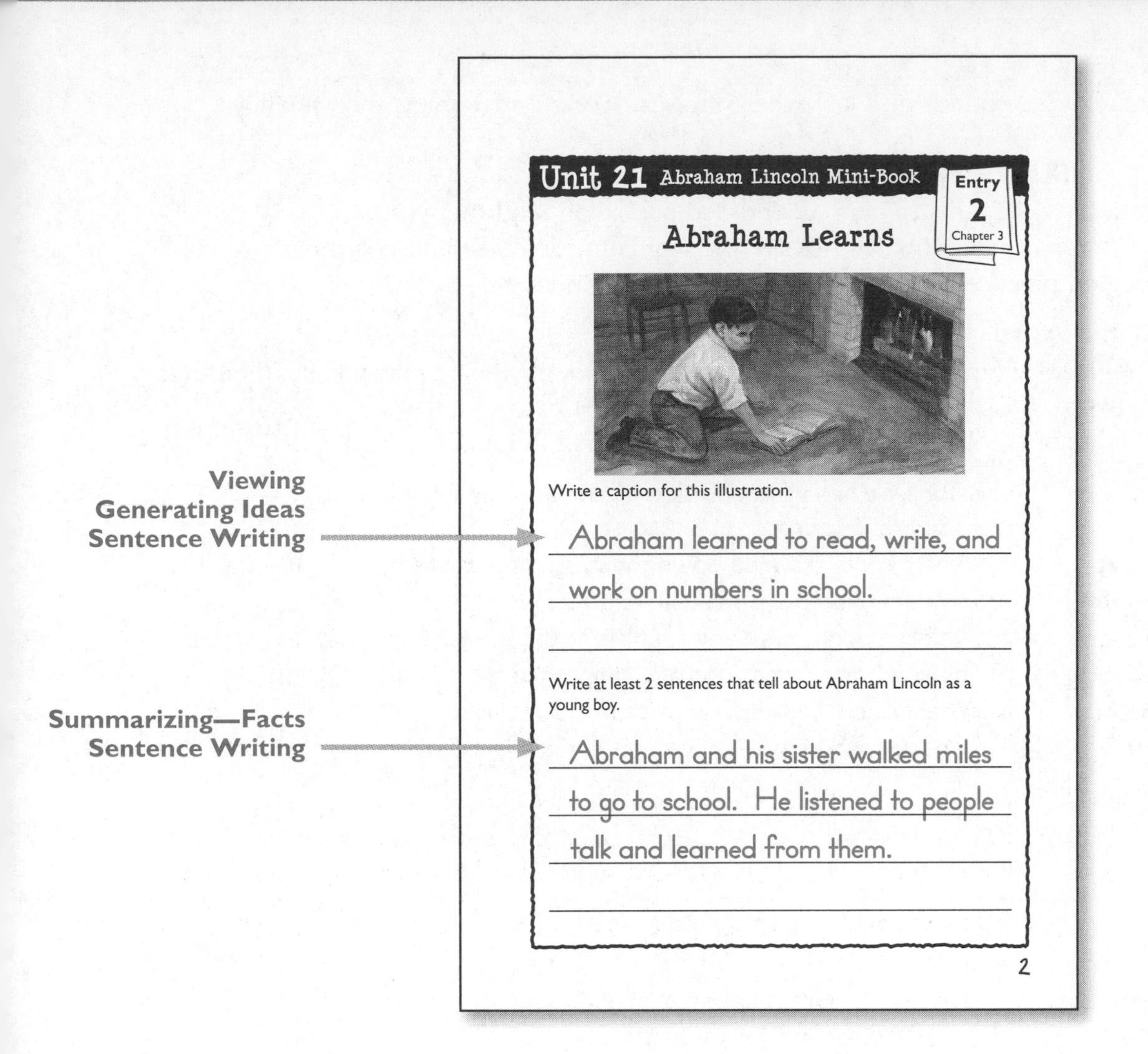

Unit 21 Abraham Lincoln Mini-Book

Entry 2 Chapter 3

Abraham Learns

Write a caption for this illustration.

Abraham learned to read, write, and work on numbers in school.

Write at least 2 sentences that tell about Abraham Lincoln as a young boy.

Abraham and his sister walked miles to go to school. He listened to people talk and learned from them.

2

Viewing
Generating Ideas
Sentence Writing

Summarizing—Facts
Sentence Writing

1 SOUND REVIEW

Have students read the sounds and key word phrases. Work for accuracy, then fluency.

2 ACCURACY AND FLUENCY BUILDING

- For each task, have students say any underlined part, then read the word.
- Set a pace. Then have students read the whole words in each task and column.
- Provide repeated practice, building accuracy first, then fluency.

C1. Multisyllabic Words

- For the list of words divided by syllables, have students read each syllable, then the whole word. Use the word in a sentence, as appropriate.
- For the list of whole words, build accuracy and then fluency.

transport	Before we had railroads, horses and wagons were used to . . . *transport* . . . things.
flatboat	Some people traveled down the Mississippi River on a . . . *flatboat.*
lawmaker	Someone who helps make laws is a . . . *lawmaker.*
general	Settlers bought food and supplies at the town's . . . *general* . . . store.
saddlebags	The cowboy carried food and supplies in his . . . *saddlebags.*
opinion	When asked, Dale always gives his . . . *opinion.*
lawyer	Someone who studies and practices law is called a . . . *lawyer.*

D1. Tricky Words

- For each Tricky Word, have students use the sounds and word parts they know to silently sound out the word. Use the word in a sentence to help with pronunciation.

suit	For the wedding, Dad put on a nice . . . *suit.*
borrowed	Imo has one skateboard that he owns and another that he . . . *borrowed.*
honest	If you don't tell lies or steal, you're . . . *honest.*
woman	A girl grows up to be a . . . *woman.*
women	Girls grow up to be . . . *women.*

- Have students go back and read the whole words in the column.

3 WORD ENDINGS

Have students read any underlined word, then the word with an ending. Use the words in sentences, as needed.

4 NAMES AND PLACES

- Tell students these are the names of people and places they will read about in the story.
- Have students use the sounds and word parts they know to figure out the words.

5 MORPHOGRAPHS AND AFFIXES

- Have students read the underlined part, then the word.
- Repeat practice with whole words, mixing group and individual turns.
  Build accuracy, then fluency.

6 GENERALIZATION: READING NEW WORDS IN PARAGRAPHS

- Have students read the paragraph silently, then out loud. Tell students to use the sounds and word parts they know to read any difficult words.
- Repeat practice, as needed.

The 16th President

Unit 21 Exercise 3

Use before Chapters 4 and 5

1. SOUND REVIEW Have students review sounds for accuracy, then for fluency.

A	-y as in fly	-y as in baby	ow as in cow	ow as in snow	all as in ball
B	-dge	oa	ph	kn	ce

2. ACCURACY/FLUENCY BUILDING For each column, have students say any underlined part, then read each word. Next, have them read the column.

A1 Mixed Practice	B1 Rhyming Words	C1 Multisyllabic Words		D1 Tricky Words
plump	ready	trans•port	transport	suit
joined	steady	flat•boat	flatboat	borrowed
owned		law•mak•er	lawmaker	honest
skinny	healthy	gen•er•al	general	woman
funny	wealthy	sad•dle•bags	saddlebags	women
afford		o•pin•ion	opinion	
law		law•yer	lawyer	

3. WORD ENDINGS Have students read any underlined word, then the word with an ending.

A	treated	educated	noticed	amazed
B	marry married		carry carried	

4. NAMES AND PLACES Have students use the sounds and word parts they know to figure out the words.

Mary Todd | New Orleans | Abraham Lincoln | New Salem

5. MORPHOGRAPHS AND AFFIXES Have students read each underlined part, then the word.

express | badly | kindness | capital | became

6. GENERALIZATION Have students read the paragraph silently, then out loud. (New words: voters, gentleman, Joshua)

Yesterday, we all voted to see who would be class president. Our teacher said, "We listened to great speeches yesterday." Then she said, "Voters of Room 17, our new class president is a fine young gentleman." Then she said my name—Joshua Thomas. I couldn't believe my ears. I had won the election!

3

BUILDING INDEPENDENCE (Reminder)

Some students will try to follow your voice instead of learning to read the sounds and words. Therefore, it is important for you to demonstrate and guide practice only as needed.

Give students many opportunities to respond without your assistance—with groups and individuals. Encourage independence.

COMPREHENSION PROCESSES

Understand, Apply

PROCEDURES

1. Introducing Vocabulary

★**transport** ★**opinion**
★**educated, adventure,**
slave

- For each vocabulary word, have students read the word by parts, then read the whole word.
- Read the student-friendly explanations to students as they follow with their fingers. Then have students use the vocabulary word by following the gray text.
- Review and discuss the photos.

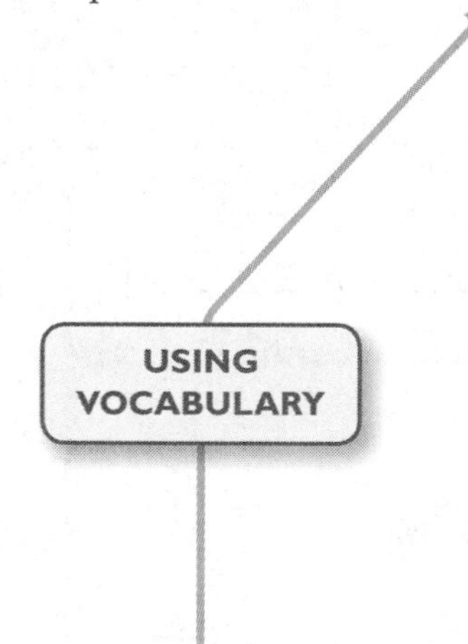

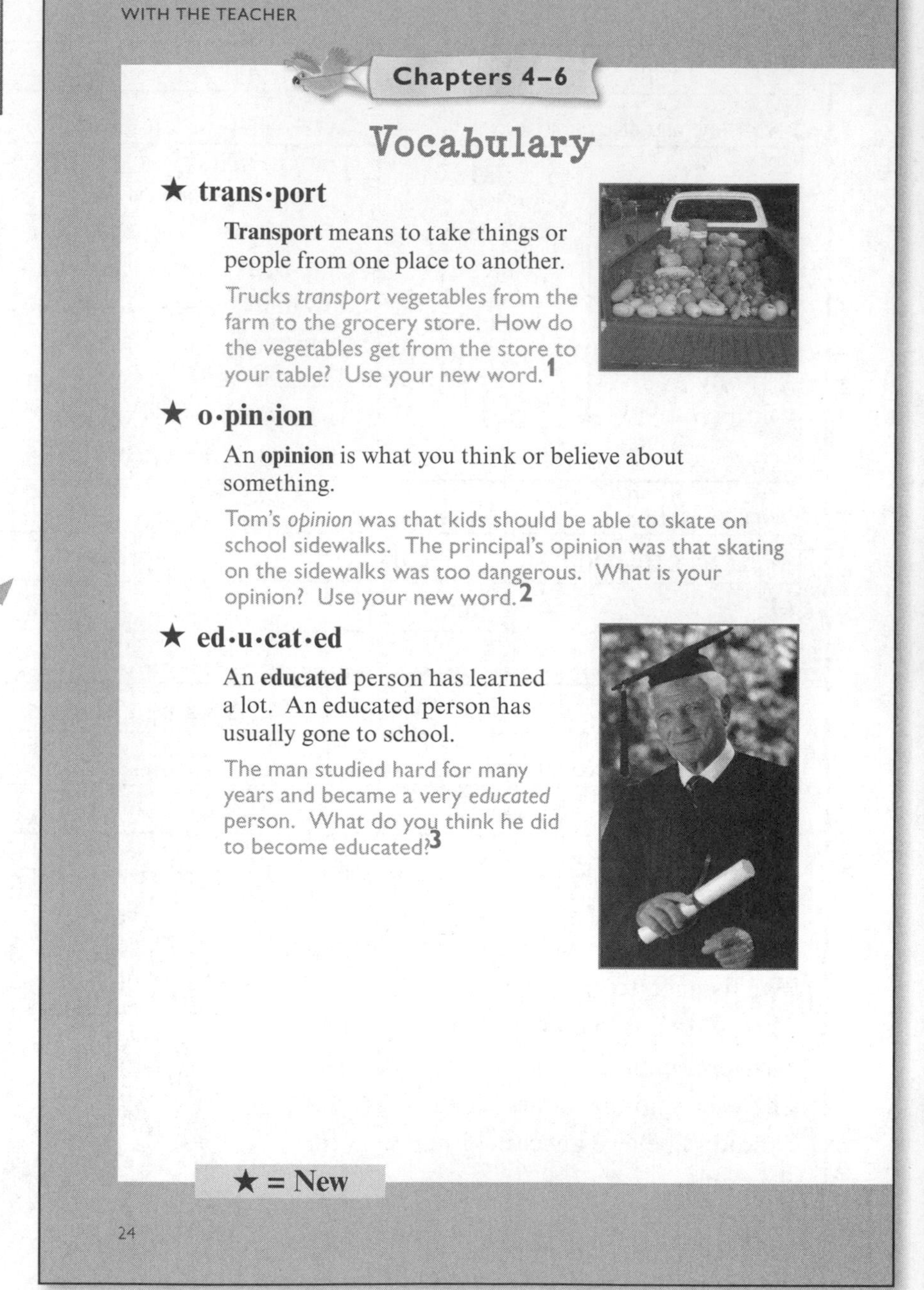

WITH THE TEACHER

Chapters 4–6

Vocabulary

★ **trans·port**

Transport means to take things or people from one place to another.

Trucks *transport* vegetables from the farm to the grocery store. How do the vegetables get from the store to your table? Use your new word.[1]

★ **o·pin·ion**

An **opinion** is what you think or believe about something.

Tom's *opinion* was that kids should be able to skate on school sidewalks. The principal's opinion was that skating on the sidewalks was too dangerous. What is your opinion? Use your new word.[2]

★ **ed·u·cat·ed**

An **educated** person has learned a lot. An educated person has usually gone to school.

The man studied hard for many years and became a very *educated* person. What do you think he did to become educated?[3]

★ = New

24

❶ **Apply:** Using Vocabulary—transport (My dad transports the vegetables from the store to our house.)

❷ **Understand:** Using Vocabulary—opinion (My opinion is that skating should be allowed on the school sidewalks.)

❸ **Apply:** Using Vocabulary—educated (The man went to school to become educated.)

★= New in this unit

2. Now You Try It!

- Read or paraphrase the directions.
- For each word, have students read the word by parts, then read the whole word.
- Have students explain or define the word in their own words. Say something like:

  Look at the word. Say the parts, then read the whole word.
  (ad•ven•ture, adventure)
  Now let's pretend that we're going to explain or define the word *adventure* to a friend. [Theo], what would you say?
  Start with "An *adventure* . . . "
  (An adventure is when you do something exciting.)
  That's right. An adventure is doing something or going somewhere new and exciting

- Have students turn to the appropriate page in the glossary and discuss how their definitions are the same or different than the glossary's. Your students may like their definitions better.

Note: By defining a word in their own words, students are demonstrating depth of word knowledge. Verbatim responses only demonstrate memorization. Encourage paraphrasing.

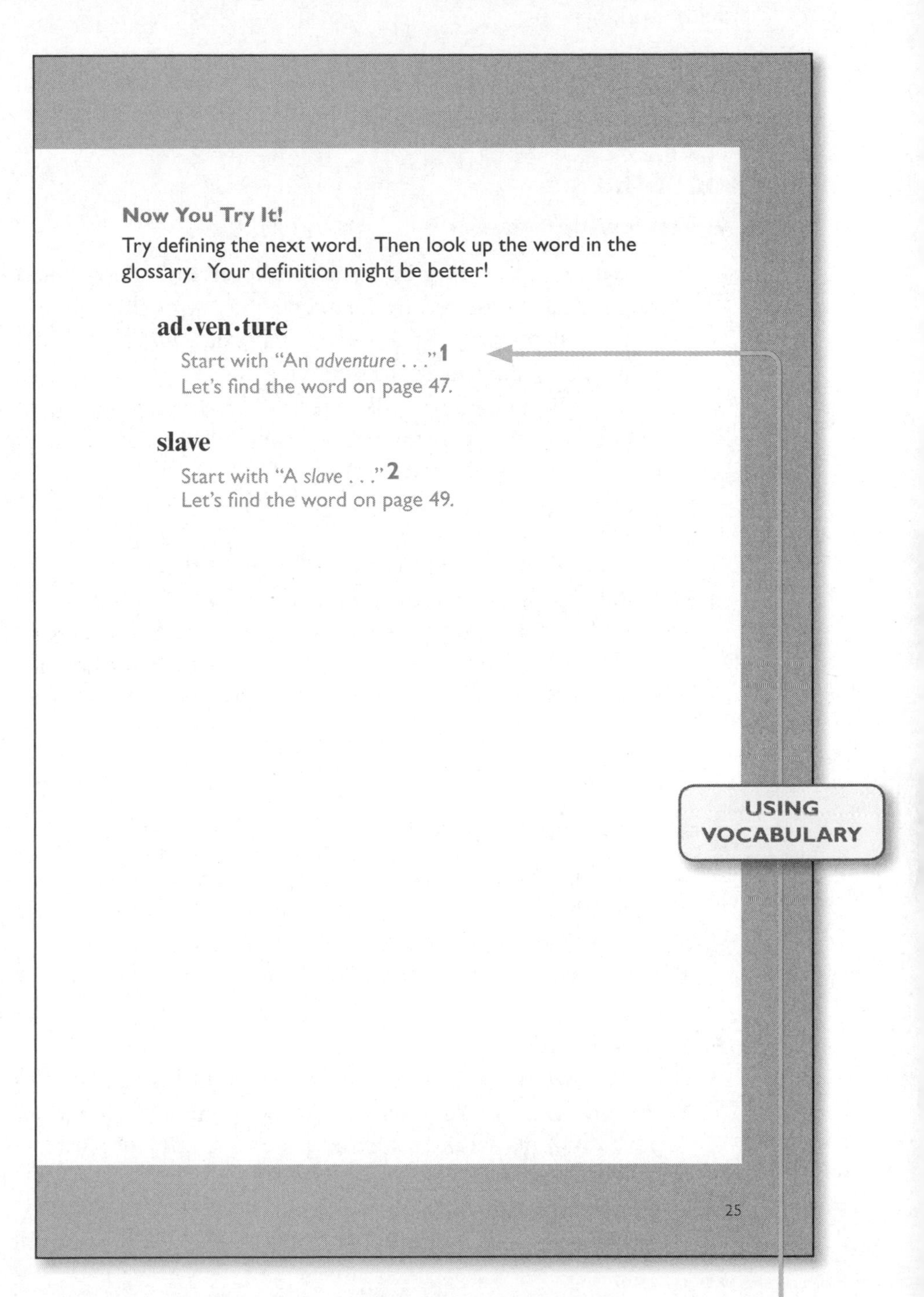
Now You Try It!
Try defining the next word. Then look up the word in the glossary. Your definition might be better!

ad•ven•ture
Start with "An *adventure* . . ."[1]
Let's find the word on page 47.

slave
Start with "A *slave* . . ."[2]
Let's find the word on page 49.

25

1. **Understand:** Defining and Using Vocabulary—adventure; Using Glossary (An adventure is doing something or going somewhere new and exciting.)
2. **Understand:** Defining and Using Vocabulary—slave; Using Glossary (A slave is someone who is owned by another person and has to work for free.)

CHAPTER 4 INSTRUCTIONS

Students read Chapter 4 with the teacher and Chapter 5 on their own.
Note: If you're working on an 8-Day Plan, you will read Chapter 5 with students.

COMPREHENSION PROCESSES

Remember, Understand, Apply

PROCEDURES

1. Reviewing Chapter 3

Summarizing; Locating Information; Inferring; Using Vocabulary—allow, permission

Review what happened in Chapter 3. Say something like:

You read Chapter 3 on your own. Let's review what you learned about Lincoln's childhood.
How did Abraham feel about school? (He liked it. He wanted to go . . .)
Let's find where the book talked about Sarah and Abraham going to school. Go back to the beginning of the chapter. Raise your hand when you find the part about Sarah and Abraham going to school. What does it say?
(Sometimes in the winter, when the farm work was done, he and Sarah were allowed to go to school.)
The book uses the word *allowed*. What does that mean? (They had permission to go.)
Did Abe and Sarah have to go to school? (no) That's right. They probably asked permission to go, and then they were *allowed*. When you ask permission to do something, you probably want to do it. That makes me think Abraham wanted to go to school.
What does the book say that leads you to think Abraham loved to read?
(He walked miles to borrow books. He said people who loaned him books were his best friends.)

2. Introducing Chapter 4

Identifying—Title; Inferring

Have students read the title. Say something like:

What is the title of the chapter? (Learning by "Littles")
What do you think that means? (He learned a little bit at a time . . .)

3. First Reading

- Ask questions and discuss the story as indicated by the gray text.
- Mix group and individual turns, independent of your voice.
  Have students work toward a group accuracy goal of 0–5 errors.
  Quietly keep track of errors made by all students in the group.
- After reading the story, practice any difficult words.
  Reread the story if students have not reached the accuracy goal.

CORRECTING DECODING ERRORS

During story reading, gently correct any error, then have students reread the sentence.

4. Second Reading, Short Passage Practice: Developing Prosody

- Demonstrate expressive, fluent reading of the first two paragraphs.
- Guide practice with your voice.
- Provide individual turns while others track with their fingers and whisper read.
- Repeat with one paragraph or page at a time.

WITH THE TEACHER

Chapter 4

Learning by "Littles"

Abraham wanted to see more of the world. At 19, he got a job on a flatboat, a large wooden boat used to transport food and goods. Abraham's first trip away from home took him down the Mississippi River to New Orleans.

Abraham had many adventures and saw many new things. In a marketplace, he saw people sold like animals. They were slaves.

Abraham wanted people to be treated with kindness and respect. Seeing human beings treated so badly made him sad and very mad. Stories say that Lincoln knew then that he wanted to help the slaves. But what could a poor farm boy do?

What made Abraham sad and very mad?[1] What did this poor farm boy want to do?[2]

26

COMPREHENSION BUILDING (Reminder)

Encourage students to answer questions with complete sentences. If students have difficulty comprehending, think aloud with them or reread the portion of the story that answers the question. Then, repeat the question.

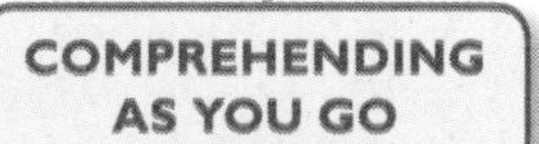

COMPREHENDING AS YOU GO

1. **Understand:** Explaining; Using Vocabulary—slavery (He saw people sold like animals. Slavery made him sad and mad.)
2. **Understand:** Explaining; Using Vocabulary—slave (Abraham Lincoln wanted to help the slaves.)

THE 16TH PRESIDENT
27

WITH THE TEACHER

Soon after this trip, Abraham left the farm. He wanted to live in a place where he could learn more and do new things. He moved to the town of New Salem, Illinois.

Lincoln worked in the general store. People were amazed at his great height. His strong hands and strong back made work easy. People liked Abraham because he told funny stories and treated everyone like a friend. Often, people talked to him about the government. Abraham listened and learned.

Abraham noticed that many important people were educated. They knew how to speak well. Abraham wanted to learn how to speak well too. He had an idea. He joined a local club where people practiced making speeches. He soon learned to speak clearly and to express his opinions.

Why did people like Abraham Lincoln?[1] How did Lincoln learn to speak well?[2]
What do you think was Lincoln's *opinion* of slavery?[3]

28

COMPREHENDING AS YOU GO

1. **Understand:** Explaining—Character Traits (Characterization) (He told funny stories and treated everyone like a friend.)
2. **Understand:** Explaining (He joined a club where people practiced making speeches.)
3. **Apply:** Inferring, Explaining; Using Vocabulary—opinion, slavery (His opinion of slavery was that it was wrong.)

THE 16TH PRESIDENT
29

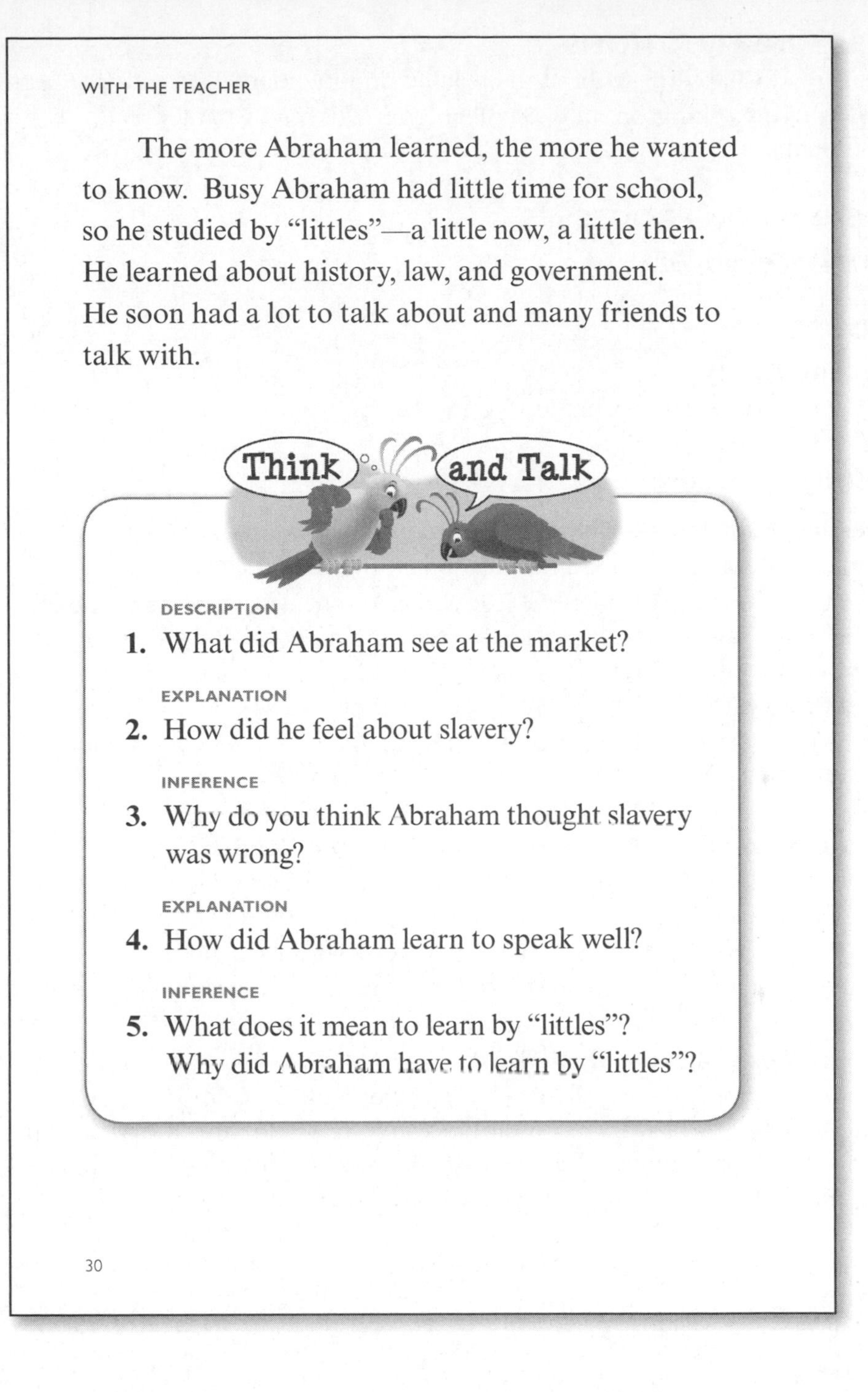

WITH THE TEACHER

The more Abraham learned, the more he wanted to know. Busy Abraham had little time for school, so he studied by "littles"—a little now, a little then. He learned about history, law, and government. He soon had a lot to talk about and many friends to talk with.

DESCRIPTION

1. What did Abraham see at the market?

EXPLANATION

2. How did he feel about slavery?

INFERENCE

3. Why do you think Abraham thought slavery was wrong?

EXPLANATION

4. How did Abraham learn to speak well?

INFERENCE

5. What does it mean to learn by "littles"? Why did Abraham have to learn by "littles"?

30

❶ **Understand:** Describing (He saw people being sold like animals.)

❷ **Understand:** Explaining (It made him mad and sad.)

❸ **Apply:** Inferring, Explaining; Using Vocabulary—**respect** (He wanted all people to be treated with kindness and respect.)

❹ **Understand:** Explaining (He joined a club where people practiced making speeches.)

❺ **Apply:** Inferring, Explaining (It means to learn a little bit here and a little bit there. Abraham had to learn by littles because he couldn't go to school every day and he didn't have a library nearby.)

CHAPTER 5 INSTRUCTIONS

Students read Chapter 5 without the teacher, independently or with partners.
Note: If you're working on an 8-Day Plan, you will read Chapter 5 with students.

COMPREHENSION PROCESSES

Understand, Apply, Analyze

PROCEDURES

1. Getting Ready

Have students turn to Chapter 5 on page 31.

2. Setting a Purpose

Inferring; Explaining—Character Traits (Characterization)

Before students begin reading, say something like:

Read the next part to find out a little about Abraham's first election, how he became a lawyer, and his marriage. Read to find out the answers to these questions:

- People voted for Abe. Did it matter that he was poor?
- What did people like about Abe? (This will tell you why people voted for Abe.)

> **PREP NOTE**
> **Setting a Purpose**
> Write questions on a chalkboard, white board, or large piece of paper before working with your small group.

3. Reading on Your Own: Partner or Whisper Reading

- Have students take turns reading every other page with a partner or have students whisper read Chapter 5 on their own.
- Continue having students track each word with their fingers.
- Have students ask themselves or their partners the gray text questions.

4. Comprehension and Skill Work

For students on a 6-Day Plan, tell them they will do Comprehension and Skill Activity 3 and work on their Lincoln Mini-Book after they read on their own. Guide practice, as needed. For teacher directions, see pages 60 and 61. (For 8-Day Plans, see the Lesson Planner, page 9.)

5. Homework 3: Repeated Reading

Chapter 5

Lincoln, the Man

People liked Abraham so much they wanted him to be one of the people who made their state laws. In his first election, Abraham did not get enough votes to win. But almost every voter in his town voted for him! He tried again two years later and won. He became a lawmaker in his state. Abraham Lincoln was on his way to becoming a leader.

ON YOUR OWN

When Abraham joined the state government, he was only 25 years old. He stood 6 feet, 4 inches tall and was as skinny as a pole. His pants were too short. His hands were very big. Even he said he was not much to look at. He needed a good suit to look like a gentleman. But he was poor.

Abe borrowed money to buy what he needed. He borrowed a horse to ride and headed off to his new life in the state capital. Everything he owned filled two saddlebags.

Abe studied law books that he borrowed from a friend. It took two years of hard work, but Abe became a lawyer. People said that Abe was an honest man and a good lawyer. He spoke well and was very clever.

How did Abraham get ready for his new job?[1]

32

COMPREHENDING AS YOU GO

1 **Understand:** Explaining (Abe studied law books.)

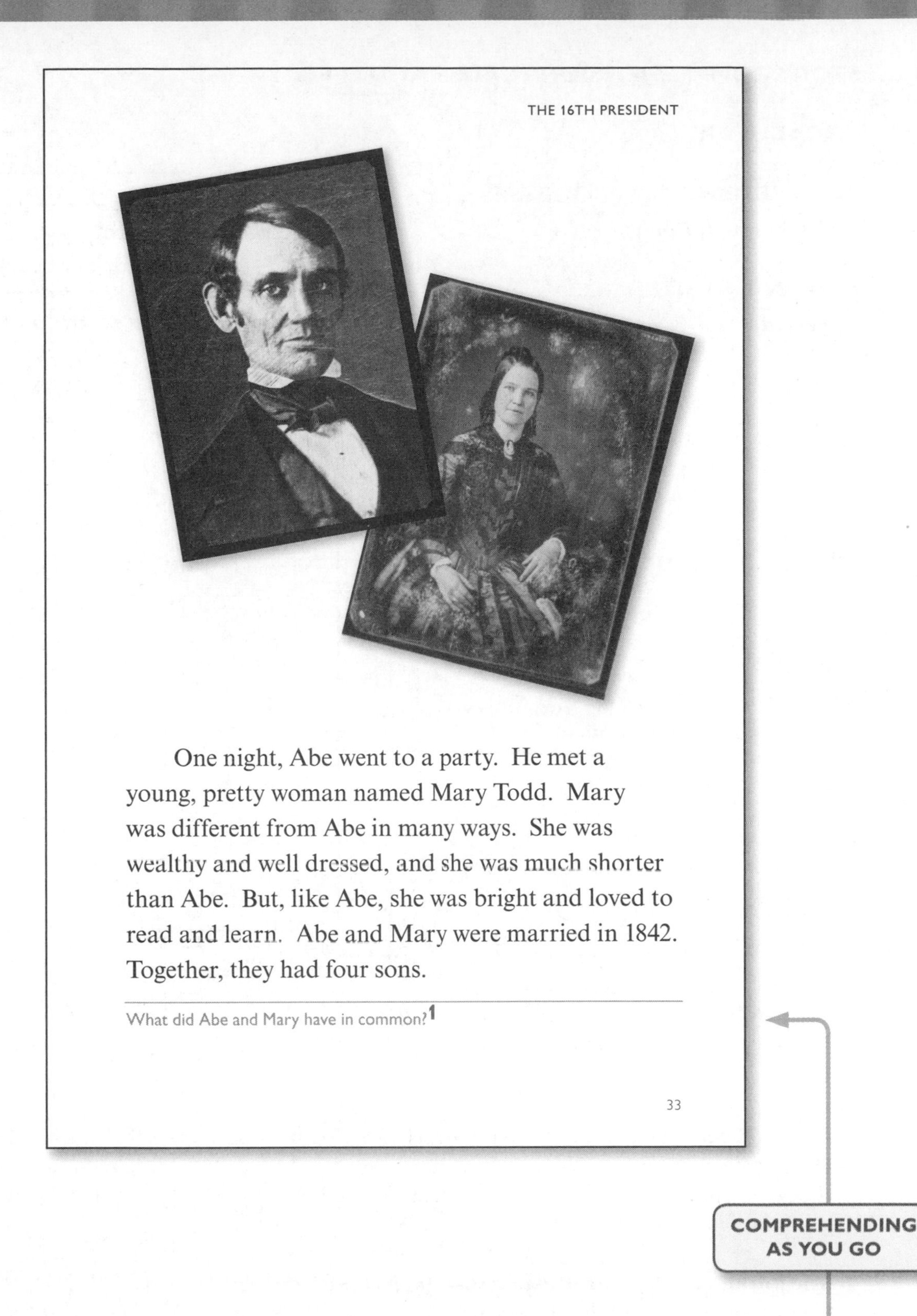

THE 16TH PRESIDENT

One night, Abe went to a party. He met a young, pretty woman named Mary Todd. Mary was different from Abe in many ways. She was wealthy and well dressed, and she was much shorter than Abe. But, like Abe, she was bright and loved to read and learn. Abe and Mary were married in 1842. Together, they had four sons.

What did Abe and Mary have in common?[1]

33

COMPREHENDING AS YOU GO

1 **Analyze:** Comparing (Abe and Mary both loved to read and learn.)

STORY COMPREHENSION • CAUSE AND EFFECT

VOCABULARY

COMPREHENSION PROCESSES

Understand, Apply

WRITING TRAITS

Period

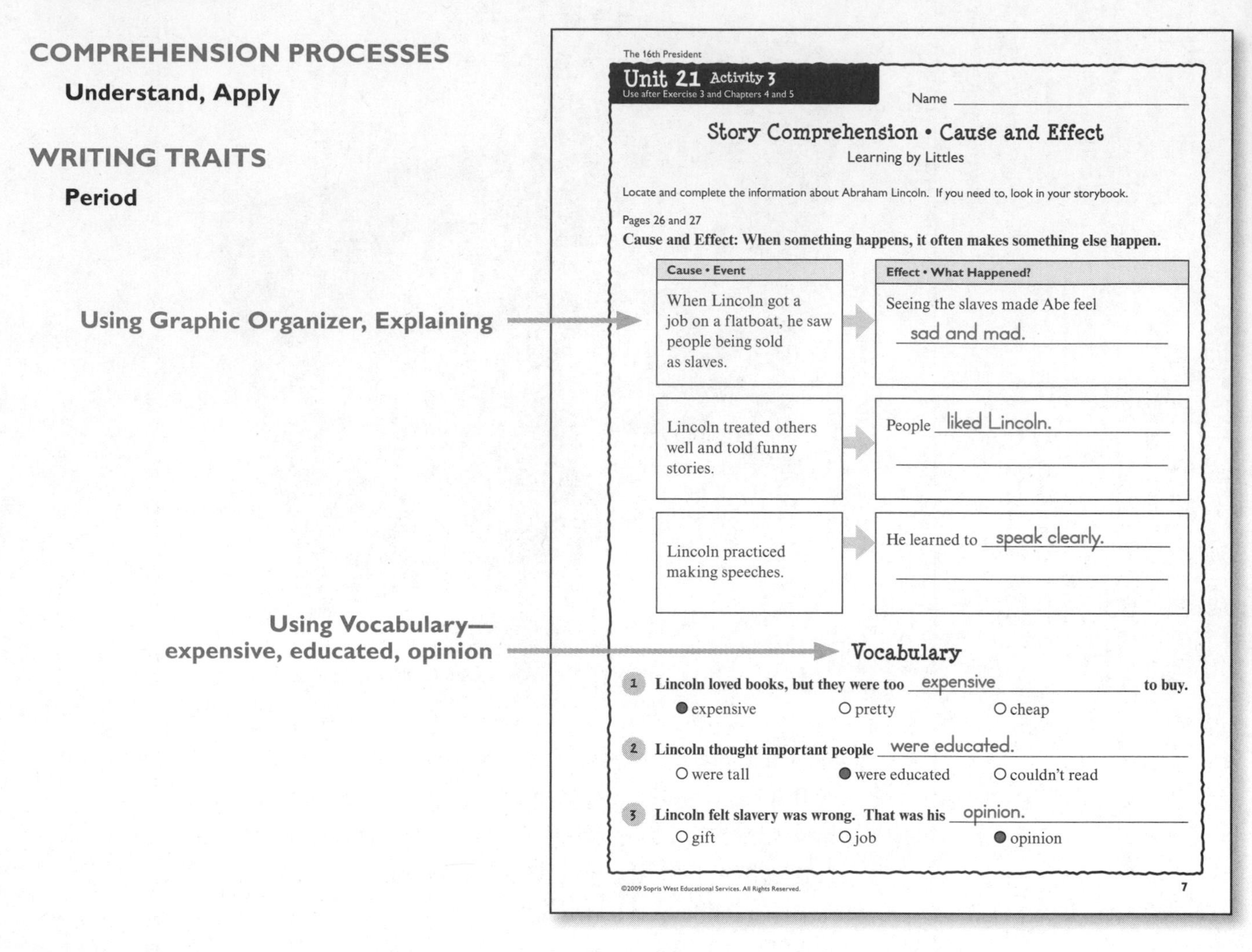

The 16th President

Unit 21 Activity 3
Use after Exercise 3 and Chapters 4 and 5

Name ______________________

Story Comprehension • Cause and Effect

Learning by Littles

Locate and complete the information about Abraham Lincoln. If you need to, look in your storybook.

Pages 26 and 27

Cause and Effect: When something happens, it often makes something else happen.

Cause • Event	Effect • What Happened?
When Lincoln got a job on a flatboat, he saw people being sold as slaves.	Seeing the slaves made Abe feel sad and mad.
Lincoln treated others well and told funny stories.	People liked Lincoln.
Lincoln practiced making speeches.	He learned to speak clearly.

Vocabulary

1. **Lincoln loved books, but they were too** expensive **to buy.**
   ● expensive ○ pretty ○ cheap
2. **Lincoln thought important people** were educated.
   ○ were tall ● were educated ○ couldn't read
3. **Lincoln felt slavery was wrong. That was his** opinion.
   ○ gift ○ job ● opinion

7

PROCEDURES

For each step, demonstrate and guide practice, as needed. Then have students complete the page independently.

Cause/Effect: Sequence Chart, Locating Information—Specific Instructions
Have students explain the outcomes by reading the boxes in the first column and completing the sentences in the second column. Remind students to look back in their storybook for information.

Vocabulary: Selection Response—Basic Instructions (Items 1–3)
Have students fill in the bubbles and blanks with the correct vocabulary word. Remind them to put a period at the end of a sentence, where needed.

Self-monitoring
Have students check and correct their work.

ENTRY 3

COMPREHENSION PROCESSES

Understand, Create

WRITING TRAITS

Ideas and Content
Word Choice
Conventions—Complete Sentence, Capital, Period
Presentation

Unit 21 Abraham Lincoln Mini-Book | Entry 3 Chapter 5

Lincoln, the Man

Write a caption for these photos.

Viewing, Generating Ideas Sentence Writing →

Abe and Mary Todd married in 1842.

Write at least 2 sentences that tell about Abraham Lincoln as a lawmaker, lawyer, husband, or father.

Summarizing—Facts; Sentence Writing →

At age 25, Abraham joined the state government. After studying for two years, he became a lawyer.

3

PROCEDURES

For each step, demonstrate and guide practice, as needed. Then have students complete the page independently.

1. Caption Writing—Basic Instructions

Have students look at the photos, then write an appropriate caption. Remind them to start their caption with a capital, use a capital for Lincoln's and Todd's names, and end with a period.

2. Paragraph Writing—Basic Instructions

- Have students write a paragraph summarizing Abraham Lincoln's life as lawmaker, lawyer, husband, and/or father. Remind them to use capitals and periods.
- Think aloud with students and brainstorm possible answers.

1 SOUND REVIEW

2 SOUND PRACTICE

- For each task, have students spell and say the focus sound in the gray bar.
- Next, have students read each underlined sound, the word, then the whole column.
- Repeat with each column, building accuracy first, then fluency.

★3 SHIFTY WORDS

Have students read the words. As needed, remind students that just one sound changes.

Be careful in this row. Just one sound changes in each word.

Read the words. (vote, wrote, rose, close, chose)

SHIFTY WORDS CORRECTION PROCEDURE

If students make an error, put the word on the board. Underline the incorrect sound.

Have students identify the difficult sound, then sound the word out smoothly. Have students read the row again. Return to the difficult word for three correct responses.

4 ACCURACY AND FLUENCY BUILDING

C1. Multisyllabic Words

- For the list of words divided by syllables, have students read each syllable, then the whole word. Use the word in a sentence, as appropriate.
- For the list of whole words, build accuracy and then fluency.

angry	The little baby's face turned red when he got . . . *angry.*
believed	Even though the story was incredible, Mindy . . . *believed* . . . it.
elected	Michelle got the most votes, so she was . . . *elected.*
Washington	The first president of the U.S. was George . . . *Washington.*
markets	Miss Tam loves shopping at the farmers' . . . *markets.*
swollen	When Brie sprained her ankle, it became . . . *swollen.*

D1. Tricky Words

- For each Tricky Word, have students use the sounds and word parts they know to silently sound out the word. Use the word in a sentence to help with pronunciation.

territories

Look at the first word. Say the word parts silently. Thumbs up when you know the word. Use my sentence to help you pronounce the word. At one time, America had many large areas of land, or . . . *territories.*

Read the word two times. (territories, territories)

terrible	When I get sick, I feel . . . *terrible.*
ideas	When people brainstorm, they're coming up with new . . . *ideas.*
nothing	Dorothea has everything she needs. She needs . . . *nothing.*

- Have students go back and read the whole words in the column.

5 WORD ENDINGS

6 MORPHOGRAPHS AND AFFIXES

7 NAMES AND PLACES

★= New in this unit

❽ GENERALIZATION: READING NEW WORDS IN PARAGRAPHS

- Have students read the paragraph silently, then out loud. Tell students to use the sounds and word parts they know to read any difficult words.
- Repeat practice, as needed.

The 16th President

Unit 21 Exercise 4

Use before Chapter 6

1. SOUND REVIEW Use selected Sound Cards from Units 1–19.

2. SOUND PRACTICE In each column, have students spell and say the sound, next say any underlined sound and the word, then read the column.

kn	ee	i_e	ou
knew	free	wife	south
knock	creek	life	about
kneel	agreed	time	aloud

★3. SHIFTY WORDS Have students read the words.

vote	wrote	rose	close	chose

4. ACCURACY/FLUENCY BUILDING For each column, have students say any underlined part, then read each word. Next, have them read the column.

A1 Mixed Review	B1 Rhyming Words	C1 Multisyllabic Words		D1 Tricky Words
laws	thought	an•gry	angry	territories
slaw	bought	be•lieved	believed	terrible
beard	ought	e•lect•ed	elected	ideas
bread	fought	Wash•ing•ton	Washington	nothing
		mar•kets	markets	
		swol•len	swollen	

5. WORD ENDINGS Have students read each underlined word, then the word with an ending.

arrived	happened	slavery	markets	shocked

6. MORPHOGRAPHS AND AFFIXES Have students read the underlined part, then the word.

nation	decided	unhappy	movable	powerful

7. NAMES AND PLACES Have students use the sounds and word parts they know to figure out the words.

Civil War	Washington	April	Americans

8. GENERALIZATION Have students read the paragraph silently, then out loud. (New words: elected, flag)

After Joshua Thomas was elected president of his class, he decided that they needed a class flag. He organized a contest. Many boys and girls made flags. The school librarian was chosen to be the judge. The winner will be announced next week.

Lawson Elementary

4

MIX IT UP (Reminder)

Response forms can be varied. Have students say the sounds using different rhythms. Have students use big voices, small voices, and deep voices. Pass the cards to students. Then have them find and return a sound. Be creative, but maintain a high rate of group responses.

CHAPTER 6 INSTRUCTIONS

Students read Chapter 6 with the teacher.

COMPREHENSION PROCESSES

Understand, Apply, Analyze

PROCEDURES

1. Reviewing Chapters 4 and 5

Inferring; Summarizing—Character Traits (Characterization)

Discuss the main character. Say something like:
In Chapter 5, you read about the start of Abraham's political career. Let's think about the questions on the board. People voted for Abe. Did it matter that he was poor? (no)
What did people like about Abe? This will tell you why people voted for Abe.
(He studied and worked hard. Even though he was poor, he did his best. He told funny stories and treated people well . . .)

2. Introducing Chapter 6

Predicting

Read and discuss the title. Say something like:
This chapter is called "Lincoln, the President."
What do you think the chapter will be about? (It will be about what Lincoln did when he was president.)

3. First Reading

- Ask questions and discuss the story as indicated by the gray text.
- Mix group and individual turns, independent of your voice.
  Have students work toward a group accuracy goal of 0–5 errors.
- After reading the story, practice any difficult words.
  Reread the story if students have not reached the accuracy goal.

4. Second Reading, Timed Readings: Repeated Reading

- As time allows, have students do Timed Readings while others follow along.
- Time individuals for 30.
- Determine words correct per minute. Record student scores.

5. Partner or Whisper Reading: Repeated Reading

Before beginning independent work, have students finger track and partner or whisper read.

6. Comprehension and Skill Work

Tell students they will do Comprehension and Skill Activity 4 and work on their Lincoln Mini-Book after they read on their own. You may also wish to assign the optional Passage Reading Fluency Activity. Guide practice, as needed. For teacher directions, see pages 70–73. (For 8-Day Plans, see the Lesson Planner, page 9.)

7. Homework 4: Repeated Reading

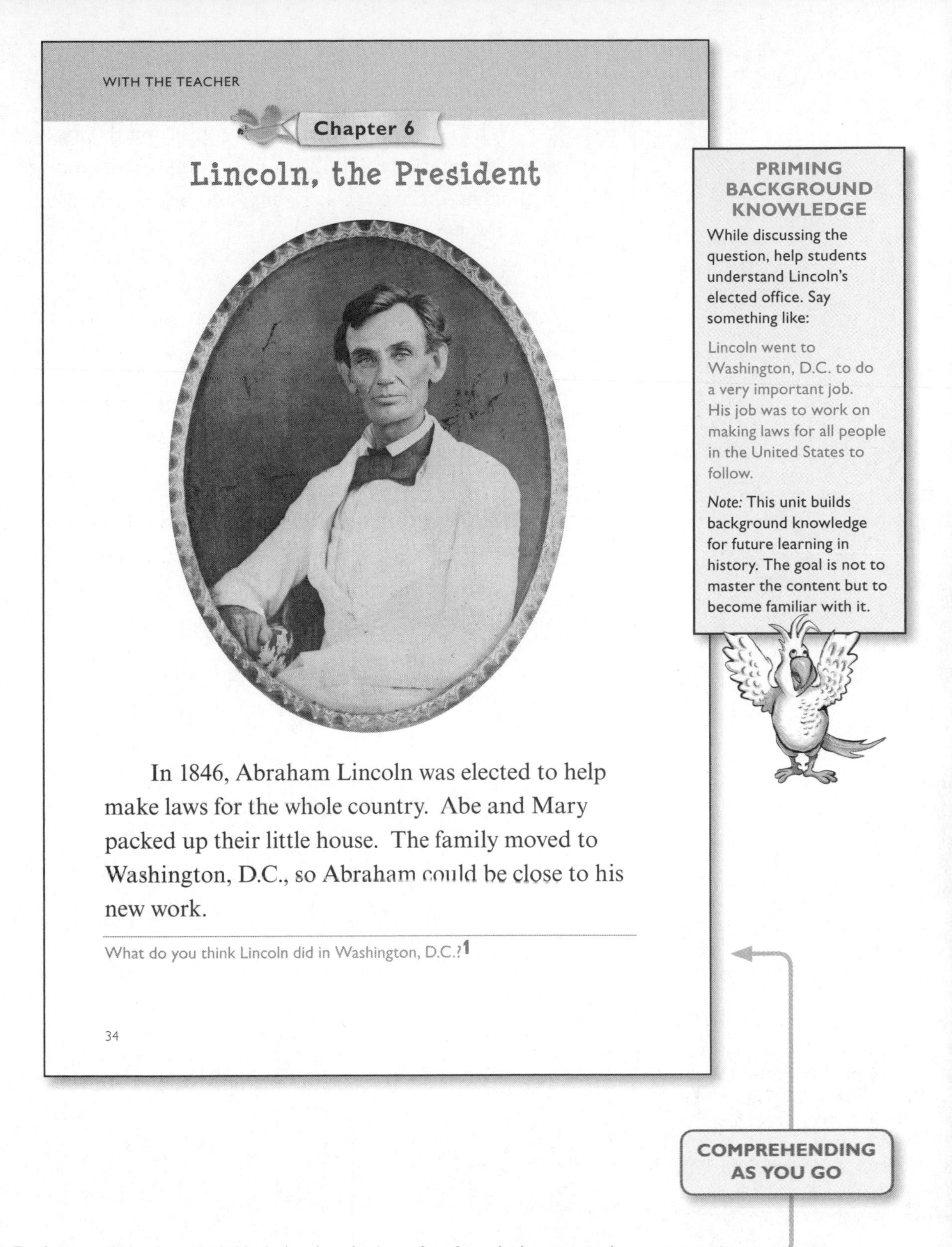

WITH THE TEACHER

Chapter 6

Lincoln, the President

In 1846, Abraham Lincoln was elected to help make laws for the whole country. Abe and Mary packed up their little house. The family moved to Washington, D.C., so Abraham could be close to his new work.

What do you think Lincoln did in Washington, D.C.?[1]

34

PRIMING BACKGROUND KNOWLEDGE

While discussing the question, help students understand Lincoln's elected office. Say something like:

Lincoln went to Washington, D.C. to do a very important job. His job was to work on making laws for all people in the United States to follow.

Note: This unit builds background knowledge for future learning in history. The goal is not to master the content but to become familiar with it.

COMPREHENDING AS YOU GO

❶ **Understand:** Explaining (Abraham Lincoln helped make laws for the whole country.)

When they arrived in the nation's capital, Abe saw slave markets. The sight upset him. Abraham still believed slavery was wrong, and he wanted it to stop. Not everyone agreed.

Americans had to find an answer to an important and difficult question. Should people be allowed to own slaves?

Abraham spoke out loud and often about his opinion. He said, "If slavery is not wrong, nothing is wrong."

People began to notice this smart and kind man. Newspapers everywhere wrote about the things he said. People all over the country knew his face and his words. Abraham Lincoln became famous.

In 1860, people asked Abraham to run for president. He was ready. "The fight must go on," he said.

What was Lincoln's opinion about slavery?[1] What did Lincoln do to become famous?[2] What did Lincoln mean by, "The fight must go on"?[3]

COMPREHENDING AS YOU GO

1. **Understand:** Explaining; Using Vocabulary—opinion, slavery (Lincoln believed that slavery was wrong.)
2. **Apply:** Inferring, Explaining; Using Vocabulary—slavery (Lincoln talked about slavery and how it was wrong. People listened, and newspapers wrote about him.)
3. **Apply:** Inferring, Explaining; Using Vocabulary—slavery (He meant that he had to keep working to end slavery.)

To win votes, Abe spent a lot of time meeting and talking with people. He shook so many hands that his own hands became sore and swollen. He also started to grow his famous beard.

Lincoln won the election. Most people think he won because of his powerful words and ideas. But maybe the beard helped too!

"Mary, we are elected," Abe told his wife one day in 1860. The new president and his family should have been happy. They were going to live in the White House. But the victory was bittersweet. People in the North and the South were upset with each other. A big problem was slavery.

People in the South felt leaders in the North were trying to push them around. Some were afraid that Lincoln might try to end slavery. One by one, states in the South decided not to be part of the United States. They formed their own country. They had their own flag. They even picked their own president.

What was the problem in the United States when Lincoln was president?[1]
Why was winning the election bittersweet?[2]

36

FOCUS ON HUMOR

After completing the page, say something like:
Why do most people think Lincoln won the election?

The story says that growing a beard may have helped Abe win the election. What do you think?

COMPREHENDING AS YOU GO

1. **Understand:** Explaining; Using Vocabulary—slavery, opinion (One big problem was slavery. People had different opinions about it.)
2. **Analyze:** Drawing Conclusions; **Apply:** Using Vocabulary—bittersweet (Winning the election was bittersweet because winning made Lincoln happy, but he was president during a bad time, which probably made him sad too.)

BUILDING BACKGROUND KNOWLEDGE

Briefly explain the map to students. Say something like:
This map shows the United States when Lincoln was alive. Pioneers were moving west. The places that are white were not yet states.

COMPREHENDING AS YOU GO

After Reading Page 36, Have Students View the Map on Page 37

1. **Apply:** Using Graphic Organizer
   States in the North are shown in blue.
   Touch the states in the North.
   States in the South are shown in gray.
   Touch the states in the South.
   Touch the states that wanted to form their own country.

WITH THE TEACHER

On April 12, 1861, a terrible thing happened. The Civil War began. Americans in the North fought Americans in the South. Friends and family fought each other. Many people died. The war lasted four long years. It made the president very sad, but he kept telling people how important it was to keep the country together.

INFERENCE, EXPLANATION

1. Lincoln was president during a difficult time. What was the problem?

DRAWING CONCLUSIONS

2. Why do you think people still talk about Lincoln and even celebrate his birthday today?

38

FOCUS ON BACKGROUND KNOWLEDGE

After reading the page, ask:
After the South left the United States and elected its own president, what happened? (There was a war between the North and the South.)

Yes, there was a war in the United States. If that happened now, it would be like people in New York being at war with people in Alabama or Florida. It is a very sad and angry time when people are at war.

❶ **Apply:** Inferring, Explaining (The Civil War began. People in the North fought people in the South.)

❷ **Analyze:** Drawing Conclusions (He was president during a war. He was an important president. He worked to end slavery, which changed the country . . .)

PASSAGE READING FLUENCY

FLUENCY

Accuracy, Expression, Rate

PROCEDURES

For each step, demonstrate and guide practice, as needed. Then have students complete the page independently.

Passage Reading—Basic Instructions

- Have students read the practice words.
- Have students finger track and whisper read the story two times—the first time for accuracy and the second time for expression. Have students cross out a log cabin each time they finish.
- Have students do a one-minute Timed Reading and cross out the timer.

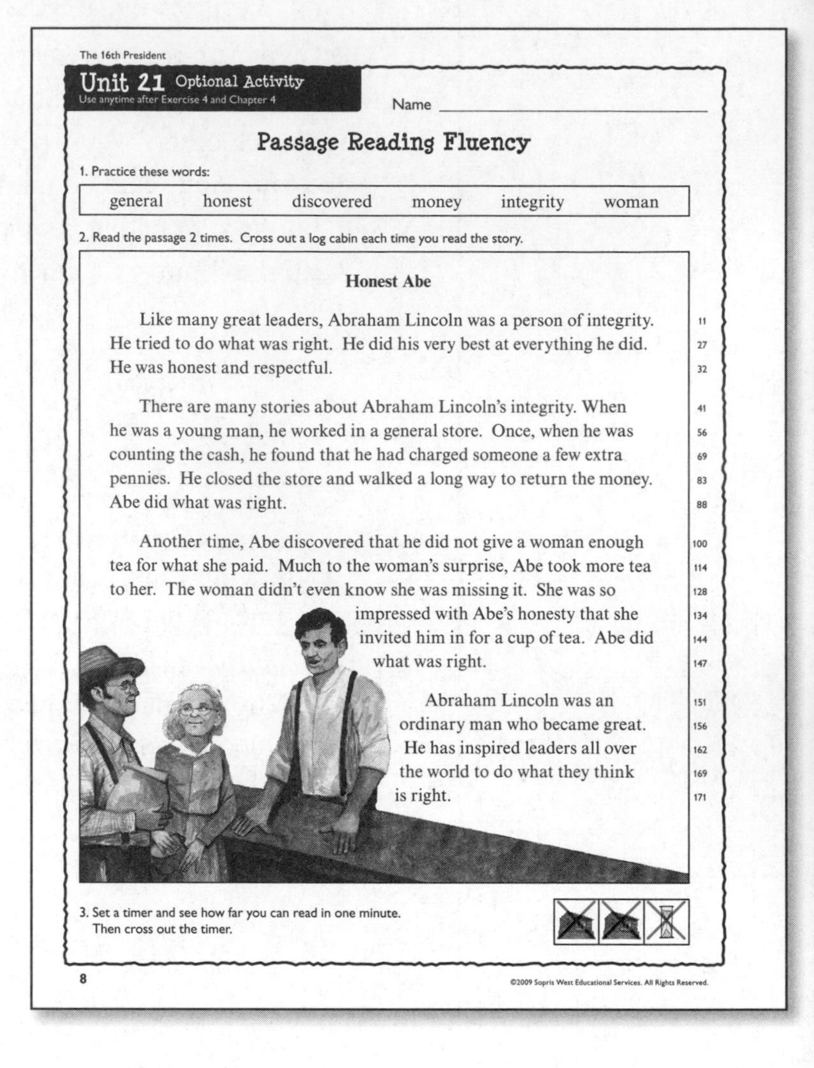

The 16th President

Unit 21 Optional Activity
Use anytime after Exercise 4 and Chapter 4

Name ______________________

Passage Reading Fluency

1. Practice these words:

general	honest	discovered	money	integrity	woman

2. Read the passage 2 times. Cross out a log cabin each time you read the story.

Honest Abe

Like many great leaders, Abraham Lincoln was a person of integrity. 11
He tried to do what was right. He did his very best at everything he did. 27
He was honest and respectful. 32

There are many stories about Abraham Lincoln's integrity. When 41
he was a young man, he worked in a general store. Once, when he was 56
counting the cash, he found that he had charged someone a few extra 69
pennies. He closed the store and walked a long way to return the money. 83
Abe did what was right. 88

Another time, Abe discovered that he did not give a woman enough 100
tea for what she paid. Much to the woman's surprise, Abe took more tea 114
to her. The woman didn't even know she was missing it. She was so 128
impressed with Abe's honesty that she 134
invited him in for a cup of tea. Abe did 144
what was right. 147

Abraham Lincoln was an 151
ordinary man who became great. 156
He has inspired leaders all over 162
the world to do what they think 169
is right. 171

3. Set a timer and see how far you can read in one minute.
Then cross out the timer.

8

©2009 Sopris West Educational Services. All Rights Reserved.

CHARACTERIZATION

LOCATING INFORMATION

COMPREHENSION PROCESSES

Understand, Apply

WRITING TRAITS

Ideas and Content
Word Choice
Conventions—Complete Sentence, Capital, Period
Presentation

Using Graphic Organizer; Describing—Character Traits (Characterization)

Describing—Character Traits (Characterization)

Inferring; Explaining
Using Vocabulary—bittersweet

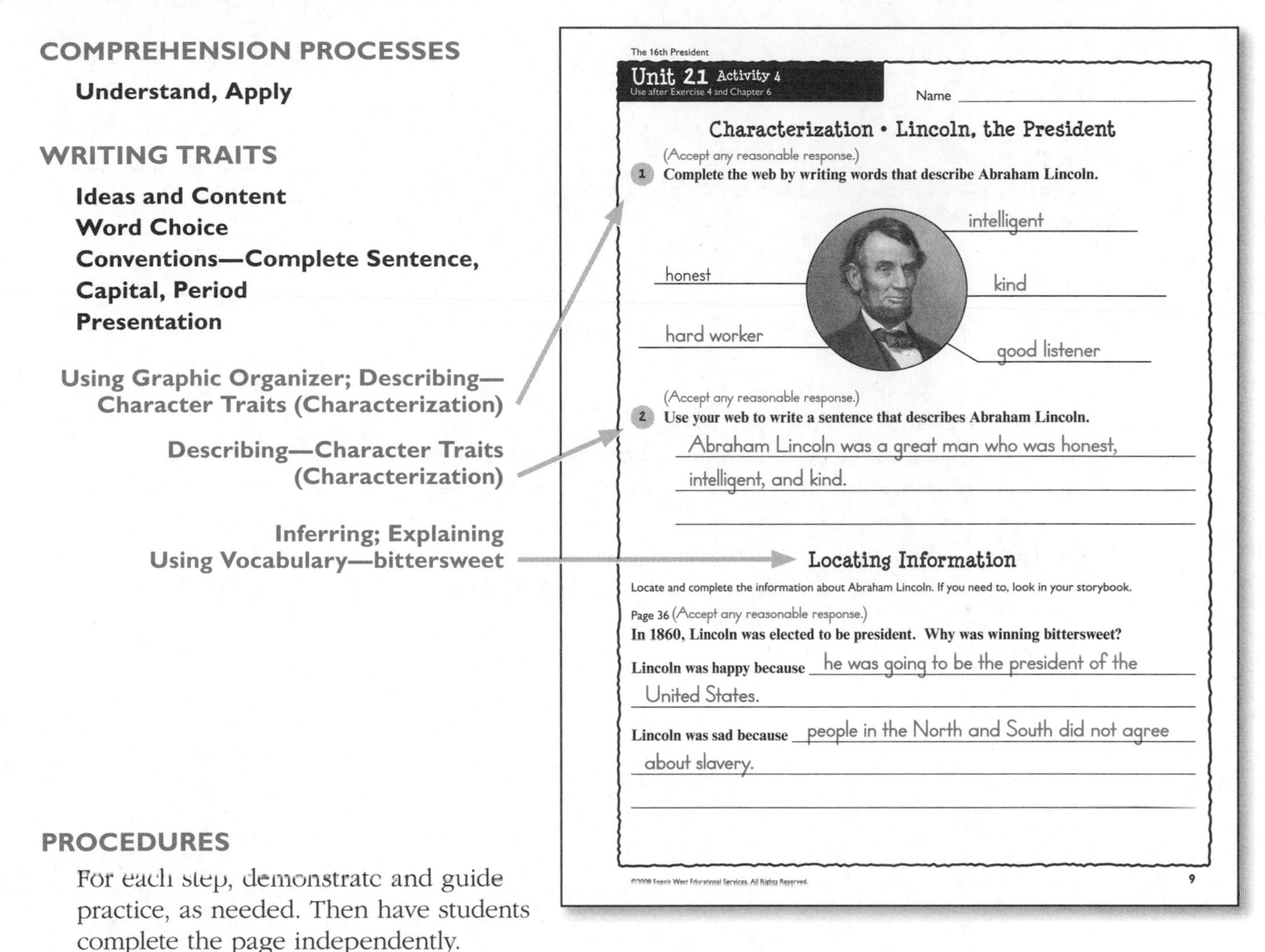

The 16th President

Unit 21 Activity 4
Use after Exercise 4 and Chapter 6

Name ______

Characterization • Lincoln, the President

(Accept any reasonable response.)

1 **Complete the web by writing words that describe Abraham Lincoln.**

intelligent
honest
kind
hard worker
good listener

(Accept any reasonable response.)

2 **Use your web to write a sentence that describes Abraham Lincoln.**

Abraham Lincoln was a great man who was honest, intelligent, and kind.

Locating Information

Locate and complete the information about Abraham Lincoln. If you need to, look in your storybook.

Page 36 (Accept any reasonable response.)

In 1860, Lincoln was elected to be president. Why was winning bittersweet?

Lincoln was happy because he was going to be the president of the United States.

Lincoln was sad because people in the North and South did not agree about slavery.

©2008 Sopris West Educational Services. All Rights Reserved.

9

PROCEDURES

For each step, demonstrate and guide practice, as needed. Then have students complete the page independently.

Characterization

1. **Web—Basic Instructions** (Item 1)
   Have students read the directions and write words or phrases on the web that describe Abraham Lincoln.

2. **Description: Sentence Writing—Specific Instructions** (Item 2)
   - Have students read the directions, then write a descriptive sentence about Abraham Lincoln. Remind students to use snazzy words if they can. Caution students that they will not be able to use all the words from their web.
   - Guide students through the activity, only as needed.

Locating Information—Specific Instructions

Have students read the directions, then complete each sentence. Remind students to look back in their storybooks if they need to.

Self-monitoring

Have students check and correct their work.

ENTRY 4

COMPREHENSION PROCESSES

Understand, Create

WRITING TRAITS

Ideas and Content
Word Choice
Conventions—Complete Sentence, Capital, Period
Presentation

PROCEDURES

For each step, demonstrate and guide practice, as needed. Then have students complete the page independently.

1. **Caption Writing—Basic Instructions**
   Have students look at the photo, then write an appropriate caption. Remind them to start their caption with a capital, use a capital for Lincoln's name, and end with a period.

2. **Paragraph Writing—Basic Instructions**
   - Have students write a paragraph summarizing Abraham Lincoln's life as president. Remind them to use capitals and periods.
   - Think aloud with students and brainstorm possible answers.

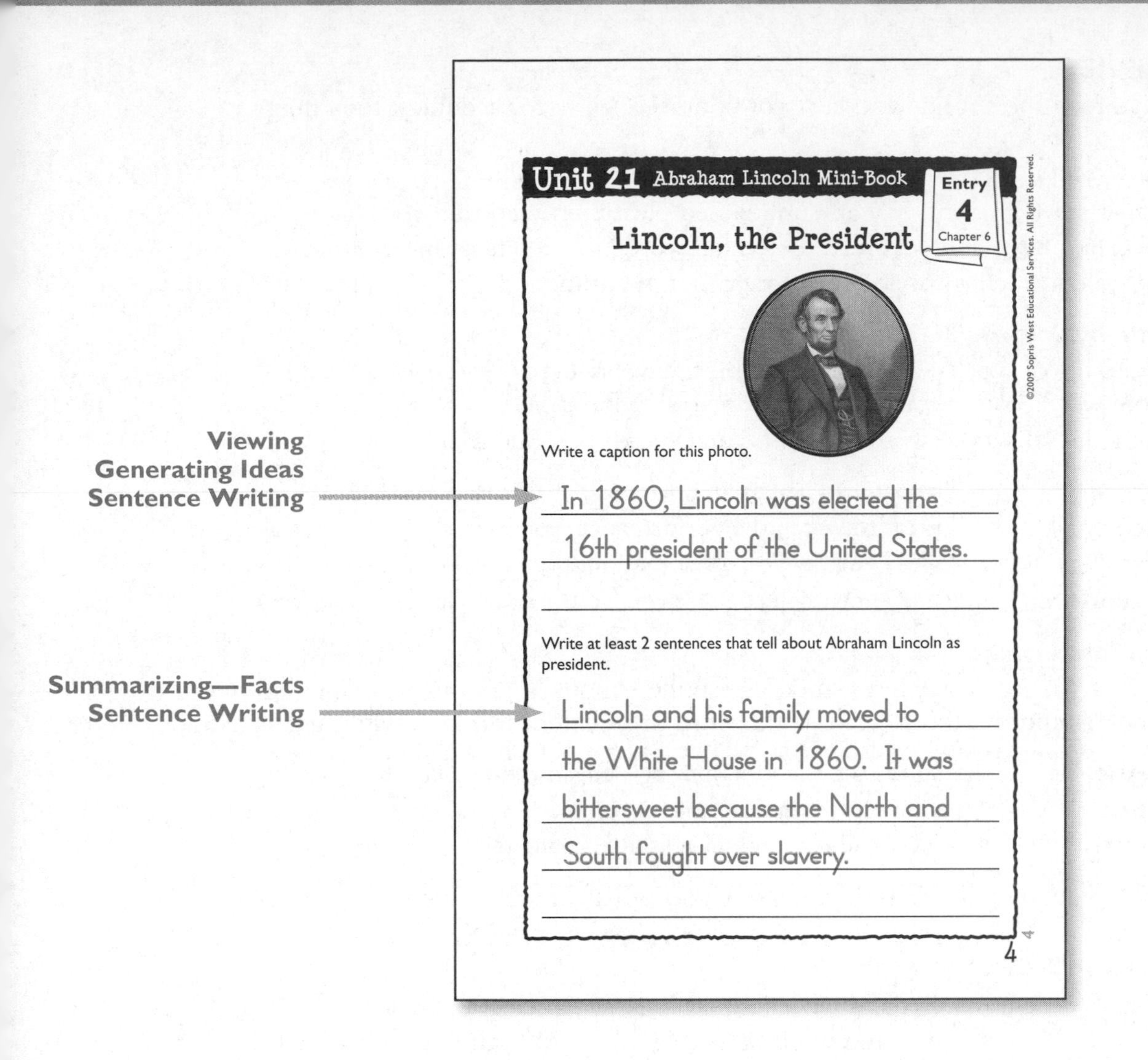

Unit 21 Abraham Lincoln Mini-Book

Entry 4 Chapter 6

Lincoln, the President

Viewing
Generating Ideas
Sentence Writing

Write a caption for this photo.

In 1860, Lincoln was elected the 16th president of the United States.

Summarizing—Facts
Sentence Writing

Write at least 2 sentences that tell about Abraham Lincoln as president.

Lincoln and his family moved to the White House in 1860. It was bittersweet because the North and South fought over slavery.

4

❶ SOUND REVIEW

Have students read the sounds and key word phrases. Work for accuracy, then fluency.

❷ ACCURACY AND FLUENCY BUILDING

- For each task, have students say any underlined part, then read the word.
- Set a pace. Then have students read the whole words in each task and column.
- Provide repeated practice, building accuracy first, then fluency.

C1. Multisyllabic Words

- For the list of words divided by syllables, have students read each syllable, then the whole word. Use the word in a sentence, as appropriate.
- For the list of whole words, build accuracy and then fluency.

theater Hannah had her ballet performance at the . . . *theater.*
balcony I want to watch the performance from high up in the . . . *balcony.*
admit When you say you did something, you . . . *admit* . . . you did it.
surrendered They knew they couldn't win, so they gave up, or . . . *surrendered.*

D1. Tricky Words

- For each Tricky Word, have students use the sounds and word parts they know to silently sound out the word. Use the word in a sentence to help with pronunciation.

fought The South and the North disagreed, so they . . . *fought.*
statue We went to the museum and saw a marble . . . *statue.*
beautiful Miss Tam said that the flowers in Hawaii were . . . *beautiful.*

- Have students go back and read the whole words in the column.

❸ NAMES AND PLACES

- Tell students these are names and places they will read about in the story.
- Have students use the sounds and word parts they know to figure out the words. Use the words in sentences, as needed.

❹ MORPHOGRAPHS AND AFFIXES

- Have students read the underlined part, then the whole word.
- Repeat practice with whole words, mixing group and individual turns. Build accuracy, then fluency.

❺ GENERALIZATION: READING NEW WORDS IN PARAGRAPHS

- Have students read the paragraph silently, then out loud. Tell students to use the sounds and word parts they know to read any difficult words.
- Repeat practice, as needed.

The 16th President

Unit 21 Exercise 5

Use before Chapter 7

1. SOUND REVIEW Have students review sounds for accuracy, then for fluency.

A	au as in astronaut	ge as in page	oi as in point	ea as in bread	ci as in circle
B	ew	aw	ue	u_e	gi

2. ACCURACY/FLUENCY BUILDING For each column, have students say any underlined part, then read each word. Next, have them read the column.

A1 Mixed Practice	B1 Word Endings	C1 Multisyllabic Words		D1 Tricky Words
joy	hated	the•a•ter	theater	fought
law	elected	bal•co•ny	balcony	statue
dreams	towering	ad•mit	admit	beautiful
place	nations	sur•ren•dered	surrendered	

3. NAMES AND PLACES Have students use the sounds and word parts they know to figure out the words.

Mr. Lincoln	John Wilkes Booth	Washington, D.C.

4. MORPHOGRAPHS AND AFFIXES Have students read the underlined part, then the word.

national	capital	rebuilt	joyful

5. GENERALIZATION Have students read the paragraph silently, then out loud. (New words: November, holiday, snuck, touchdown)

It was November, Thanksgiving holiday weekend, and the neighborhood kids were gathered at the park to play a game of football. It was the Tigers against the Lions. The Tigers were behind until the last play of the day, when Sarah snuck in for a touchdown. "Yeah," shouted the Tigers. "We never gave up. We never quit!"

GRADUALLY INCREASE STUDENT RESPONSE RATE (Reminder)

After students are accurate, gradually increase the rate of response. Demonstrate and guide a pace slightly faster than the students' rate.

COMPREHENSION PROCESSES

Understand, Apply

PROCEDURES

Introducing Vocabulary

★surrender, courage ★towering

- For each vocabulary word, have students read the word by parts, then read the whole word.
- Read the student-friendly explanations to students as they follow with their fingers. Then have students use the vocabulary word by following the gray text.
- Review and discuss the illustrations.

"The key to a successful vocabulary program is to use both formal and informal encounters so that attention to vocabulary is happening any time and all the time" (McKeown & Beck, p. 21, 2004).

Encourage students to use vocabulary words from *Read Well 2* throughout the day. Here are some suggestions for keeping words alive in your classroom.

Thumbs Up: When a student spontaneously uses a new vocabulary word, give the student a thumbs up.

Vocabulary Stars: Keep a list of vocabulary words on a bulletin board or chart. When you hear a student use a word, put his or her name and a star next to the word.

Rotate words from previous units in and out of practice.

Vocabulary Stars

opinion ★Markus ★Leilani
impressive ★Yvonne ★Tamar
inspiring ★Brady ★Navjeet

★= New in this unit

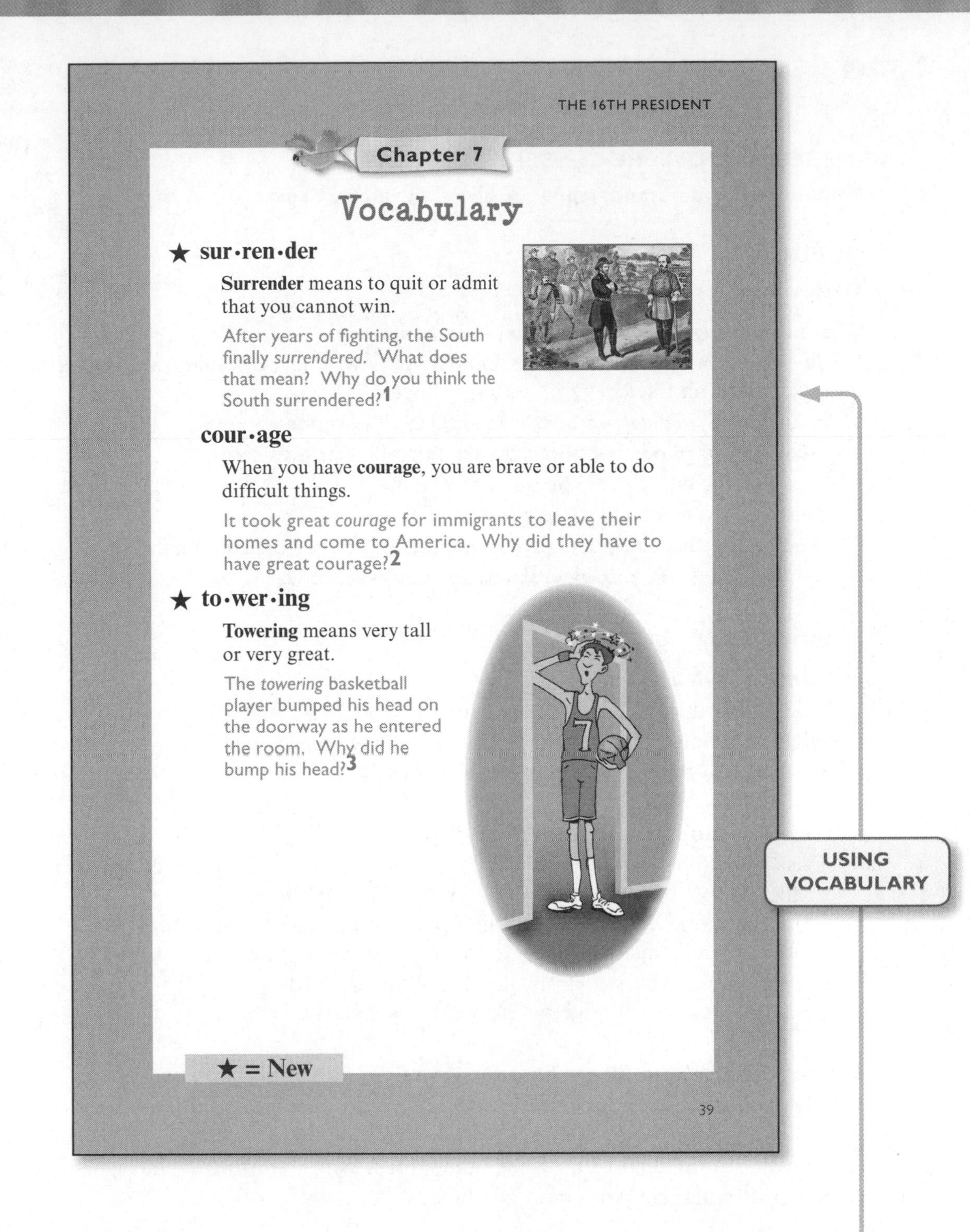

THE 16TH PRESIDENT

Chapter 7

Vocabulary

★ **sur·ren·der**

Surrender means to quit or admit that you cannot win.

After years of fighting, the South finally *surrendered.* What does that mean? Why do you think the South surrendered?[1]

cour·age

When you have **courage**, you are brave or able to do difficult things.

It took great *courage* for immigrants to leave their homes and come to America. Why did they have to have great courage?[2]

★ **to·wer·ing**

Towering means very tall or very great.

The *towering* basketball player bumped his head on the doorway as he entered the room. Why did he bump his head?[3]

★ = New

39

❶ **Understand:** Defining and Using Vocabulary—surrender (It means the South quit. The South surrendered because the people did not think they could win.)

❷ **Apply:** Using Vocabulary—courage, immigrant (The immigrants needed courage to cross the ocean and come to a new place. Moving to a new place is hard. You need courage . . .)

❸ **Apply:** Using Vocabulary—towering (The basketball player bumped his head because he is very tall. He is a towering basketball player.)

CHAPTER 7 INSTRUCTIONS

Students read Chapter 7 with the teacher.

COMPREHENSION PROCESSES

Remember, Understand, Apply, Analyze, Evaluate, Create

PROCEDURES

1. Reviewing Chapter 6

Summarizing; Using Vocabulary—slave, slavery

Have students turn to page 34. Quickly review what happened in Chapter 6. Say something like:

In Chapter 6, we learned a little about Lincoln's presidency.
What do you remember about the time that he was president?
(The country was at war. Some people wanted slaves. Others felt it was wrong.)
That's right. The country was at war.
The South wanted to be its own country. It was a very difficult time.
Some people wanted to own slaves, but others felt it was wrong.

> **CORRECTING DECODING ERRORS**
> During story reading, gently correct any error, then have students reread the sentence.

2. Introducing Chapter 7

Identifying—Title; Inferring

Discuss the title. Say something like:

What's the title of this chapter? (Lincoln, Remembered)
What do you think this chapter will be about? (what we remember about Lincoln . . .)

3. First Reading

- Ask questions and discuss the story as indicated by the gray text.
- Mix group and individual turns, independent of your voice.
  Have students work toward a group accuracy goal of 0–6 errors.
  Quietly keep track of errors made by all students in the group.
- After reading the story, practice any difficult words.
  Reread the story if students have not reached the accuracy goal.

4. Second Reading, Short Passage Practice: Developing Prosody

- Demonstrate expressive, fluent reading of the first two paragraphs.
- Guide practice with your voice.
- Provide individual turns while others track with their fingers and whisper read.
- Repeat with one paragraph at a time.

5. Partner or Whisper Reading: Repeated Reading

Before beginning independent work, have students finger track and partner or whisper read.

6. Comprehension and Skill Work

Tell students they will do their Lincoln Mini-Book Entry 5a and 5b after they read Chapter 7. Guide practice, as needed. For teacher directions, see page 84. (For 8-Day Plans, see the Lesson Planner, page 9.)

7. Homework 5: Repeated Reading

WITH THE TEACHER

Chapter 7

Lincoln, Remembered

With the country at war, it was a hard time for Mr. Lincoln and for the United States. Still, the president knew that people had many things to be thankful for. On October 3, 1863, he created a "national day of Thanksgiving." Every year, on the fourth Thursday in November, most Americans celebrate this joyful holiday.

Who started Thanksgiving Day? 1 What do we have to be thankful for? 2

40

MAKING CONNECTIONS

Drawing Conclusions

After completing the page, say something like:

I think it's interesting that Lincoln started the Thanksgiving holiday.

Abe Lincoln helped get rid of slavery in the United States. Is that something that people in the United States are thankful for? Why? (Yes. We are thankful that no one is a slave in the United States because people can't own other people.)

He also started a holiday to help people in the United States remember they have much to be thankful for. I think President Lincoln was a wise man.

COMPREHENDING AS YOU GO

1. **Understand:** Explaining (Abraham Lincoln started Thanksgiving.)
2. **Create:** Generating Ideas (We are thankful for having food to eat. We are thankful for our families and friends . . .)

In 1864, Mr. Lincoln was re-elected president. The North and South were still at war. In January 1865, a new law was passed to end slavery.

On April 9, 1865, the South's biggest army surrendered. The war ended soon after. Abraham Lincoln could smile again, but he knew his work was not done. He wanted the United States to become a strong and healthy nation again.

The theater where Lincoln died

Not long after this, Lincoln went to see a play. People clapped as the president came into the theater. He was a hero.

Why was Lincoln finally able to smile?[1] Why was he a hero?[2]

COMPREHENDING AS YOU GO

1. **Apply:** Inferring, Explaining (He could smile because the war was over.)
2. **Analyze:** Drawing Conclusions; **Apply:** Using Vocabulary—slavery (He was a hero because he helped pass a law to end slavery. He worked to keep the country together . . .)

Not everyone loved Lincoln. John Wilkes Booth was an actor. He hated the way the war had ended. While the play was going on, he snuck into the balcony where Abe was sitting and shot him. The president died the next morning. He was 56 years old.

John Wilkes Booth

On April 15, 1865, the United States lost a great man. His life ended too soon, but people all over the world remember this towering man. People remember that he fought for what he believed was right. People remember that he helped end slavery in the United States. People remember that he kept the country together.

To help everyone remember Abraham Lincoln, the Lincoln Memorial was built in Washington, D.C. It is beautiful and huge, just like Mr. Lincoln's dreams for the United States.

What do people remember Abraham Lincoln for?[1]

COMPREHENDING AS YOU GO

1 **Understand:** Explaining; Using Vocabulary—slavery (They remember him because he fought for what he believed in and helped end slavery. He kept the country together.)

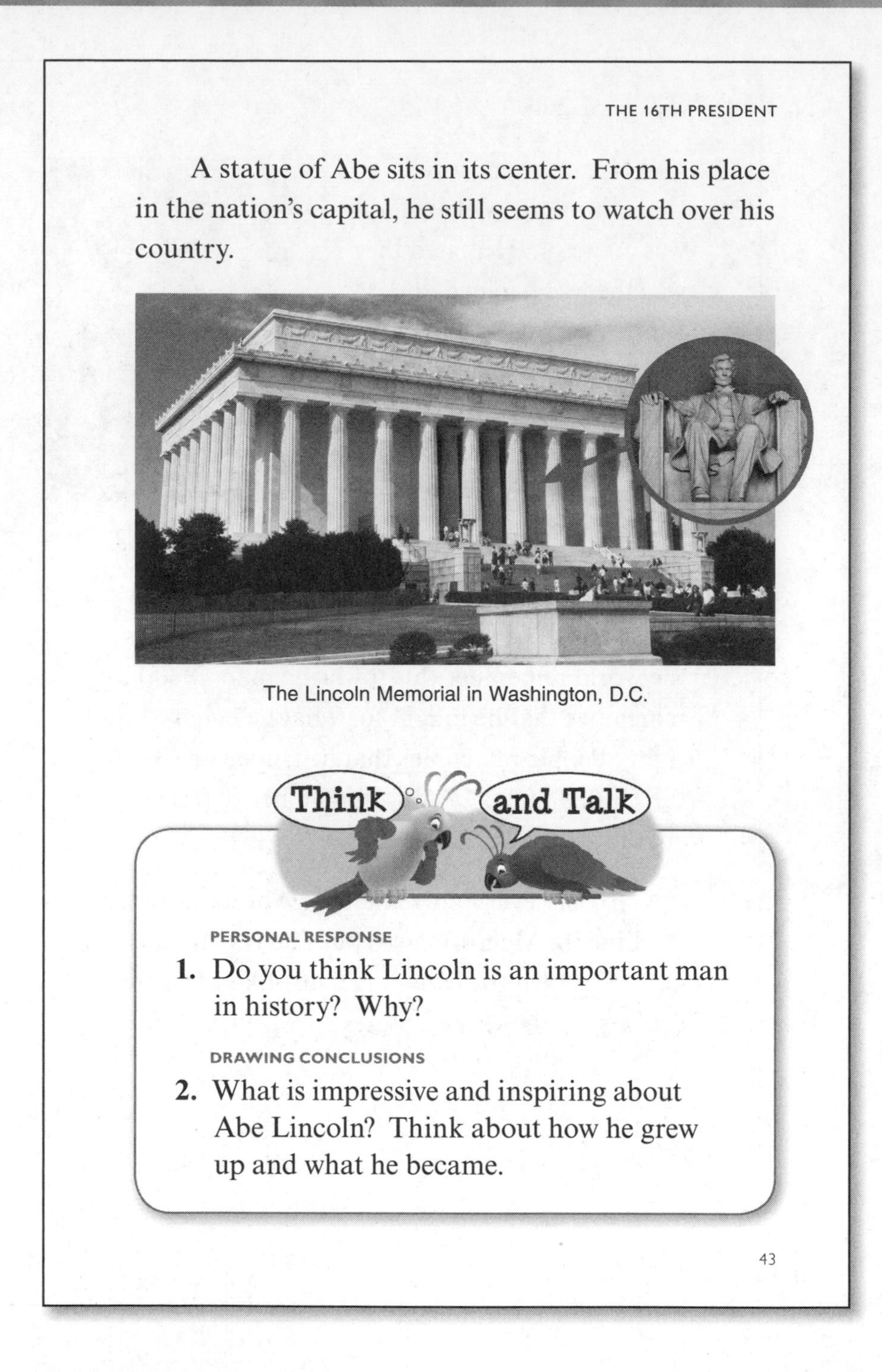

THE 16TH PRESIDENT

A statue of Abe sits in its center. From his place in the nation's capital, he still seems to watch over his country.

The Lincoln Memorial in Washington, D.C.

Think and Talk

PERSONAL RESPONSE

1. Do you think Lincoln is an important man in history? Why?

DRAWING CONCLUSIONS

2. What is impressive and inspiring about Abe Lincoln? Think about how he grew up and what he became.

43

❶ **Evaluate:** Responding; **Apply:** Using Vocabulary—slavery (Yes, he's very important. Ending slavery was very important to the United States. He kept the country together.)

❷ **Analyze:** Drawing Conclusions; **Apply:** Using Vocabulary—impressive, inspiring (Abe Lincoln is impressive because he started out with almost nothing and ended up as a great president. He always did what he thought was right. He was honest and kind. He was an inspiring man. He was a great man . . .)

JUST FOR FUN • IF I WERE . . .

The 16th President

Unit 21 Just for Fun
Use anytime after Chapter 6

Name ____________________

Just for Fun

If I were President . . .

Draw a picture of yourself as President Nancy Wing

(Accept any reasonable response.)

Write what you would do if you were the president **of your country.**

If I were the president of the United States, I would make sure no one would be hungry. I would give everyone books so they could learn to read!

10

HOW TO USE "JUST FOR FUN" ACTIVITIES

Note: This activity is optional and is *just for fun.*
Use the activity:

- as a cushion activity
- for homework
- just for fun

PROCEDURES

As time allows, have students choose what kind of leader they would be (president, queen, emperor), then fill in the blanks with their choice. Have students draw a picture of themselves as that leader, then write a paragraph about what they would do.

This page may be given to students as homework.

ENTRIES 5a, 5b

COMPREHENSION PROCESSES

Understand, Create

WRITING TRAITS

Ideas and Content
Word Choice
Conventions—Complete Sentence, Capital, Period
Presentation

PROCEDURES

For each step, demonstrate and guide practice, as needed. Then have students complete the page independently.

1. **Caption Writing—Basic Instructions**
   Have students look at the photo, then write an appropriate caption. Remind them to start their caption with a capital, use a capital for Lincoln's name, and end with a period.

2. **Personal Response: Paragraph Writing—Specific Instructions**
   - Have students write a paragraph telling why Lincoln was or was not a great man. Remind them to use capitals and periods.
   - Think aloud with students and brainstorm possible answers.

3. **Personal Response: Creative Writing—Specific Instructions**
   Have students write a sentence explaining why they would or would not have voted for Lincoln. Encourage students to use snazzy vocabulary words in their writing. Remind them to start sentences with a capital and end with a period.

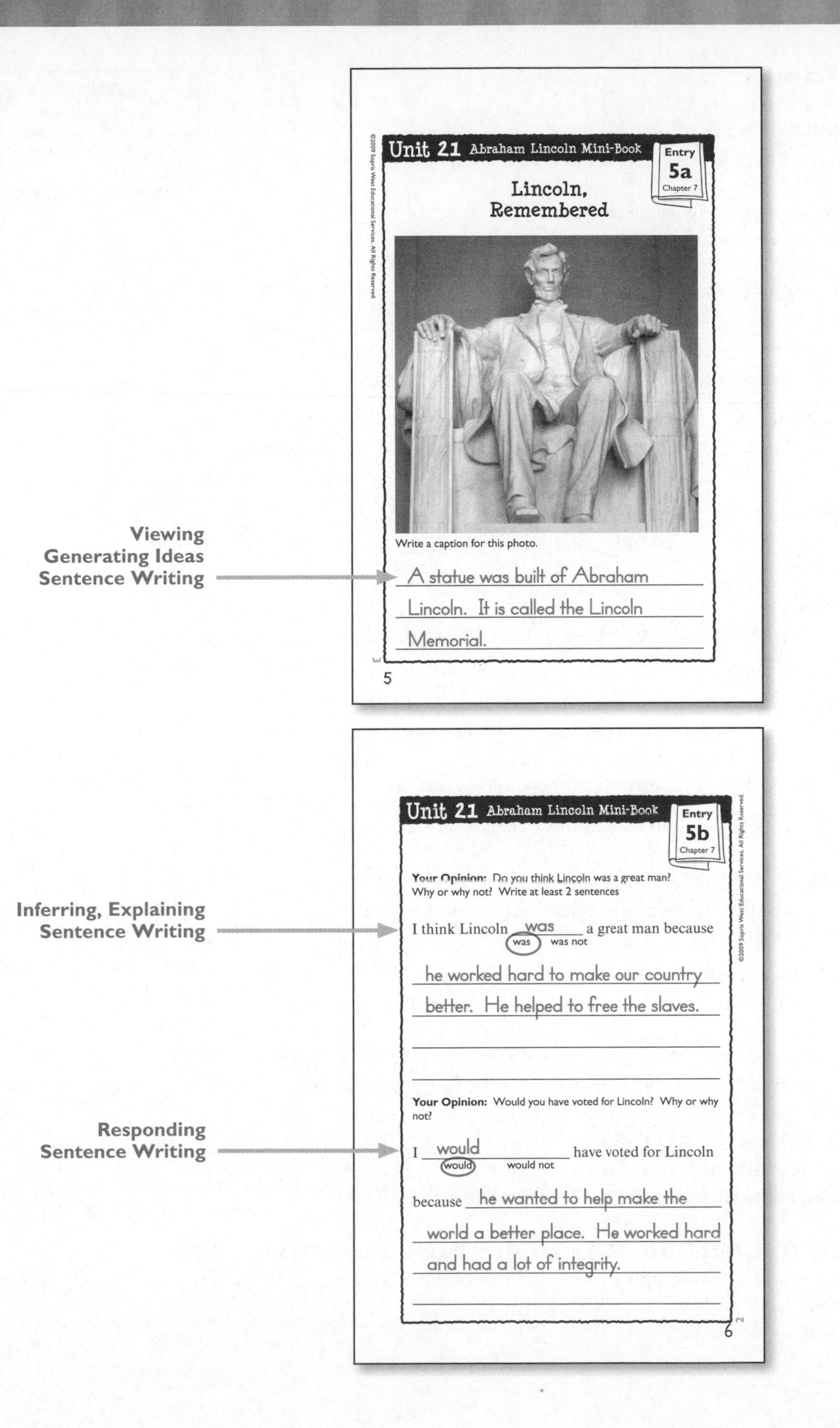

Viewing
Generating Ideas
Sentence Writing

Inferring, Explaining
Sentence Writing

Responding
Sentence Writing

Unit 21 Abraham Lincoln Mini-Book — Entry 5a, Chapter 7

Lincoln, Remembered

Write a caption for this photo.

A statue was built of Abraham Lincoln. It is called the Lincoln Memorial.

5

Unit 21 Abraham Lincoln Mini-Book — Entry 5b, Chapter 7

Your Opinion: Do you think Lincoln was a great man? Why or why not? Write at least 2 sentences

I think Lincoln was (was / was not) a great man because he worked hard to make our country better. He helped to free the slaves.

Your Opinion: Would you have voted for Lincoln? Why or why not?

I would (would / would not) have voted for Lincoln because he wanted to help make the world a better place. He worked hard and had a lot of integrity.

6

PACING

Exercise 6a should take about 10 minutes, allowing about 10 minutes for the Focus Lesson.

❶ SOUND REVIEW

❷ SHIFTY WORDS

Have students read the words. As needed, remind students that just one sound changes.

Be careful in this row. Just one sound changes in each word.

Read the words. (space, face, race, Grace, grade)

❸ ACCURACY AND FLUENCY BUILDING

- For each task, have students say any underlined part, then read the word.
- Set a pace. Then have students read the whole words in each task and column.
- Provide repeated practice, building accuracy first, then fluency.

B1, C1. Word Endings

Have students read any underlined word, then the word with an ending.

D1. Names

- Tell students these are names they will read in the story.
- Have students use the sounds and word parts they know to sound out the words. Assist, as needed.

E1. Tricky Words

- For each Tricky Word, have students use the sounds and word parts they know to silently sound out the word. Use the word in a sentence to help with pronunciation.

received Antonio got a gift. He . . . *received* . . . a gift.
women There was one restroom for men and one for . . . *women.*
young The opposite of old is . . . *young.*
thought He was thinking and thinking. He was deep in . . . *thought.*

- Have students go back and read the whole words in the column.

❹ MULTISYLLABIC WORDS

For each word, have students read the syllables, then the whole word. Use the word in a sentence, as appropriate.

husbands The opposite of wives is . . . *husbands.*
platform Abe wanted to be seen when he delivered his speech, so he stood on a . . . *platform.*
history I like learning about things in the past, so my favorite subject is . . . *history.*
suggested I asked for her advice, then I did what she . . . *suggested.*

❺ MORPHOGRAPHS AND AFFIXES

- Have students read the underlined part, then the word.
- Repeat practice with whole words, building accuracy, then fluency.

❻ GENERALIZATION: READING NEW WORDS IN PARAGRAPHS

- Have students read the paragraph silently, then out loud. Tell students to use the sounds and word parts they know to read any difficult words.
- Repeat practice, as needed.

Fluency

Unit 21 Exercise 6a

Use before Exercise 6b and Changing the Face of History

1. SOUND REVIEW Use selected Sound Cards from Units 1–19.

2. SHIFTY WORDS Have students read the words.

space	face	race	Grace	grade

3. ACCURACY/FLUENCY BUILDING For each column, have students say any underlined part, then read each word. Next, have them read the column.

A1 Mixed Practice	B1 Word Endings	C1 Word Endings	D1 Names	E1 Tricky Words
glimpse	hope	mailed	Bedell	received
spread	hoping	kissed	Abraham	women
crowd	vote	growing	November	young
change	voting	elected	October	thought
cheek	lady		Lincoln	
proud	ladies			

4. MULTISYLLABIC WORDS Have students read each word part, then read each whole word.

A	hus•bands	husbands	plat•form	platform
B	his•tor•y	history	sug•gest•ed	suggested

5. MORPHOGRAPHS AND AFFIXES Have students read the underlined word part, then the word.

important	station	community	quickly

6. GENERALIZATION Have students read the paragraph silently, then out loud. (New words: thrilled, whiskers)

I received a kitten for my birthday yesterday. I am so happy and thrilled. My kitten is bicolored and really cute. I think I will name her Whiskers because she has very long whiskers around her mouth. Mom says it is a perfect name.

6

SHIFTY WORDS CORRECTION PROCEDURE

If students make an error, put the word on the board. Underline the incorrect sound.

Have students identify the difficult sound, then sound the word out smoothly. Have students read the row again. Return to the difficult word for three correct responses.

MONITORING PROGRESS

For all activities, mix group and individual turns to keep students engaged and to monitor individual performance.

USING GRAPHIC ORGANIZER • TIMELINE

FOCUS LESSON
Skills and Strategies

PURPOSE

The purpose of this lesson is to provide explicit instruction in how to use a timeline to explain events in history. The lesson prepares students for discussing their mini-book timeline with parents.

PACING

Exercise 2b should take 10–15 minutes.

PREP NOTES

This is an oral lesson, so no overhead is needed.

COMPREHENSION PROCESSES

Remember, Understand, Apply, Analyze

PROCEDURES

1 INTRODUCTION

Using Graphic Organizer; Explaining; Defining and Using Vocabulary—approximately; Identifying—Events

- Have students review what a timeline shows. Say something like:
  Look at Exercise 6b. What do you see? (a timeline)
  What do timelines tell us? (Timelines tell us when things happened.)
- Have students make connections with the time period.
  Earlier, we studied Young America—the United States in the 1800s.
  That was approximately 200 years ago. What does *approximately* 200 years ago mean?
  (It was about 200 years ago.)
- Have students identify each event about Lincoln's life.
  Lincoln lived in the 1800s. This timeline shows three events in his life. Let's go through the timeline and touch each of those events. Touch the first event about Lincoln.
  What does it show? (It shows when Lincoln was born.) When did that happen? (1809)

2 SEQUENCING EVENTS

Using Graphic Organizer; Identifying—What; Priming Background Knowledge; Drawing Conclusions

Have students make connections between stories read earlier and Lincoln's life.
Now let's use the timeline to tell what was happening during Lincoln's lifetime.
This was an amazing time in history. Touch the year Lincoln was born.
Now touch "Buffalo Hunt." What year did that story take place? (1835)
So, what do you know about the American Indians of the Plains when Lincoln was born?
(They hunted the buffalo.)

Now look at the year Lincoln was elected president.
Were people moving across the United States in wagon trains? (yes)
Yes, our story "Life on the Trail" happened in 1843. That was when Lincoln was 34 years old.

What happened in 1863? (The Great Railroad was built.) When did Lincoln die? (1865)
Wow, so what was Lincoln doing in 1863? (He was president.)
Yes, Lincoln was president when the Great Railroad was built, and he died just two years after it was completed.

❸ SUMMARIZING

Summarizing—Events; Sequencing; Using Vocabulary—inspiring

- To prepare students for discussing the timeline at home, have them summarize each event.
  Let's review the 1800s. What happened in 1809? Use the snazzy word *inspiring*.
- Congratulate students on their scholarship.

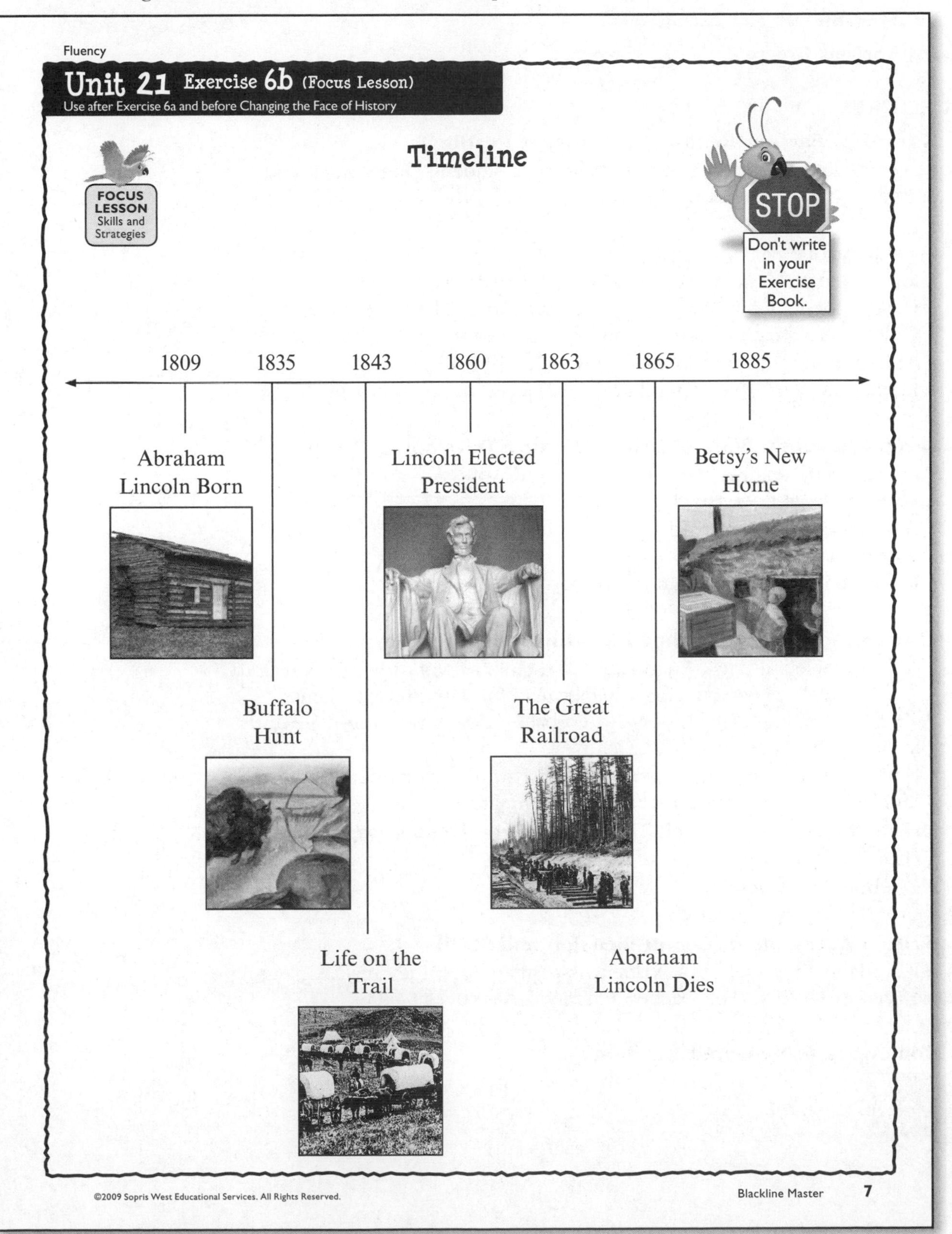

FLUENCY PASSAGE INSTRUCTIONS

This Story Reading targets fluency as the primary goal of instruction and practice.
Students do repeated readings to improve accuracy, expression, and rate.

COMPREHENSION PROCESSES

Apply, Analyze, Create

PROCEDURES

1. **Warm-Up: Partner Reading or Whisper Reading**
   Before beginning group Story Reading, have students finger track and partner or whisper read the selection.

2. **First Reading**
   - Mix group and individual turns, independent of your voice. Have students work toward a group accuracy goal of 0–4 errors. Quietly keep track of errors made by all students in the group.
   - After reading the story, practice any difficult words. Reread the story if students have not reached the accuracy goal.

3. **Second Reading, Short Passage Practice: Developing Prosody**
   - Demonstrate reading the first stanza with expression and fluency. Have students finger track as you read.
   - Have students choral read the first stanza. Encourage reading with expression and fluency.
   - Repeat with second stanza.

4. **Third Reading, Group Timed Readings: Repeated Reading**
   - Select a page. Encourage each child to work for a personal best. Have students whisper read for a one-minute Timed Reading. Tell students to go back to the top of the page and keep reading until the minute is up.
   - Have students put their finger on the last word they read and count the number of words read correctly in one minute.
   - Have students do a second Timed Reading of the same page.
   - Have students try to beat their last score.
   - Celebrate improvements.

5. **Written Assessment (Comprehension and Skill)**
   Tell students they will do a Written Assessment after they read "Changing the Face of History." For teacher directions, see pages 94–96.

6. **Homework 6: Repeated Reading**

WITH THE TEACHER

Fluency

Changing the Face of History

by L.J. Sellers
illustrated by Larry Johnson

Grace Bedell at age 14

When eleven-year-old Grace Bedell saw a picture of skinny Abraham Lincoln, she got an idea. She really wanted him to be president, and she thought she knew how to help.

Grace sat down and wrote Lincoln a letter. In the letter, she told him his face was too thin. Then she suggested that he grow a beard. It was a spunky thing for a young girl to tell an important man! Grace told Lincoln that ladies like whiskers. At that time, women couldn't vote. Grace thought that women could talk their husbands into voting for Lincoln—if only he had a beard.

When eleven-year-old Grace Bedell saw a	8
picture of skinny Abraham Lincoln, she got an	16
idea. She really wanted him to be president, and	25
she thought she knew how to help.	32
Grace sat down and wrote Lincoln a letter.	40
In the letter, she told him his face was too thin.	51
Then she suggested that he grow a beard. It	60
was a spunky thing for a young girl to tell an	71
important man! Grace told Lincoln that ladies	78
like whiskers. At that time, women couldn't	85
vote. Grace thought that women could talk	92
their husbands into voting for Lincoln—if only	100
he had a beard.	104

Grace promised Lincoln that she would get everyone she knew to vote for him if he grew a beard. She mailed her letter to Lincoln in October 1860.

Seven days later, Grace received a letter from Lincoln. She was so thrilled! Lincoln asked Grace if people would think that he was silly for growing a beard.

News about Lincoln's letter spread quickly through Grace's town. The community was so proud of Grace! Then on November 7, Abraham Lincoln was elected the 16th president of the United States.

On his way to the capital, the new president stopped in Grace's town. Grace waited at the train station with a crowd of people, hoping for a glimpse of Lincoln. She would soon get more than that.

Line	Word count
Grace promised Lincoln that she would get	7
everyone she knew to vote for him if he grew a	18
beard. She mailed her letter to Lincoln in	26
October 1860.	28
Seven days later, Grace received a letter	35
from Lincoln. She was so thrilled! Lincoln	42
asked Grace if people would think that he was	51
silly for growing a beard.	56
News about Lincoln's letter spread quickly	62
through Grace's town. The community was	68
so proud of Grace! Then on November 7,	76
Abraham Lincoln was elected the 16th president	83
of the United States.	87
On his way to the capital, the new president	96
stopped in Grace's town. Grace waited at the	104
train station with a crowd of people, hoping for	113
a glimpse of Lincoln. She would soon get more	122
than that.	124

What did Grace Bedell suggest to Lincoln in her letter?[1]

COMPREHENDING AS YOU GO

[1] **Understand:** Explaining (She told Lincoln he should grow a beard. She thought the ladies would talk their husbands into voting for Lincoln if he had a beard. She thought he would look better with a beard.)

WITH THE TEACHER

When Abraham Lincoln got off the train, he asked for Grace Bedell. Everyone stared at her. 8 16

Grace hurried to the platform. Then she saw that Lincoln had taken her advice and grown a full beard! Grace got yet another surprise. The new president bent down and kissed her cheek. Grace felt very special. In a small way, she helped change the face of history. 23 31 39 46 55 64

Do you think Grace helped get Lincoln elected?[1] How did Lincoln treat Grace?[2] What would you say to Lincoln if you could meet him today?[3]

46

COMPREHENDING AS YOU GO

1. **Analyze:** Drawing Conclusions; **Apply:** Using Vocabulary—respect (Yes, Lincoln looked older and better with a beard. It made some people like him and vote for him. No, people would have voted for Lincoln with or without the beard because they respected him.)
2. **Apply:** Inferring, Explaining (He made her feel special. He went out of his way to say thank you.)
3. **Create:** Generating Ideas (I would say "Thanks for ending slavery." I would say "I'm glad you loved to read and learn and became president." I would say "I'll vote for you if you run for president again . . .")

WRITTEN ASSESSMENT (1 of 3)

COMPREHENSION PROCESSES

Remember, Understand, Apply, Analyze, Create

WRITING TRAITS

Word Choice
Conventions—Complete Sentence, Capital, Period, Question Mark
Presentation

Unit 21 Written Assessment
Name Joseph
Date 4-16
Helen Keller

Test Taking →

Unit 21 Written Assessment
Use after Exercise 6 and Changing the Face of History

WARM-UP

graduate	college	communicate

Someone who cannot see is blind.
Someone who cannot hear is deaf.

Helen Keller

Helen Keller was born in a sleepy little town in the South. When she was born, Helen could hear and see like other children. Helen and her parents were very happy.

When Helen was a year and a half old, she became very sick. The doctor wasn't sure if Helen would live. Helen got well, but she couldn't see or hear.

For many years, Helen lived in a dark and silent world. Then Helen's parents hired a teacher named Annie. Annie knew how to talk with her fingers. Annie taught Helen how to finger spell. For the first time in many years, Helen could communicate. She learned how to read and write. She became the first deaf and blind person to graduate from college.

Helen wanted to help blind people. She wrote articles about how to prevent blindness. Helen wrote books about her life. The books helped people understand what it was like to be deaf and blind.

Helen was an inspiring person. She spoke with people all over the world. She went to the White House. She met artists, actors, and musicians. Helen made a difference in the world. She helped change the way deaf and blind children were treated. She gave people hope.

continued

94

WRITTEN ASSESSMENT (2 of 3)

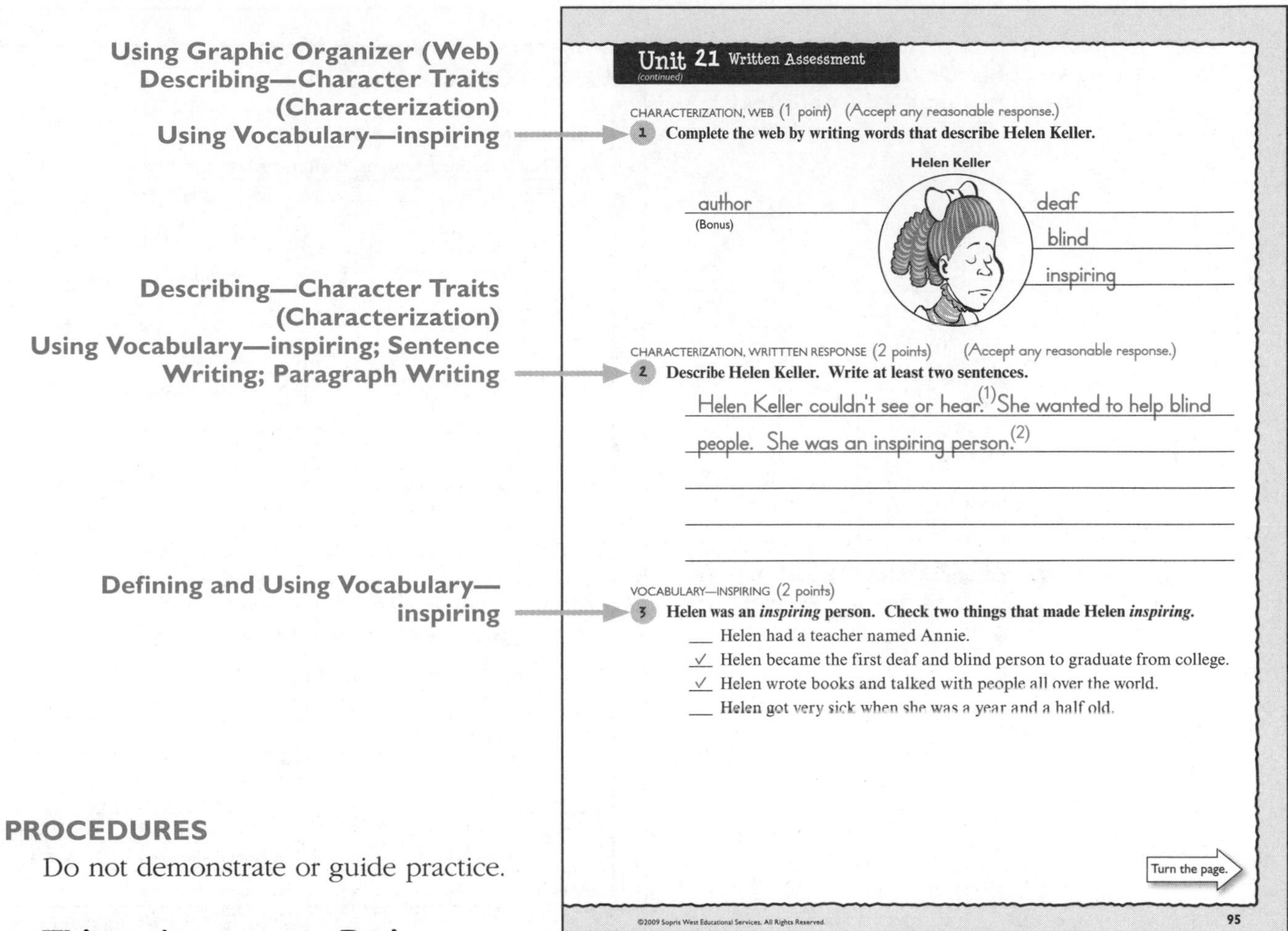

Unit 21 Written Assessment
(continued)

CHARACTERIZATION, WEB (1 point) (Accept any reasonable response.)

1 **Complete the web by writing words that describe Helen Keller.**

Helen Keller

author (Bonus)

deaf

blind

inspiring

CHARACTERIZATION, WRITTEN RESPONSE (2 points) (Accept any reasonable response.)

2 **Describe Helen Keller. Write at least two sentences.**

Helen Keller couldn't see or hear.(1) She wanted to help blind people. She was an inspiring person.(2)

VOCABULARY—INSPIRING (2 points)

3 **Helen was an *inspiring* person. Check two things that made Helen *inspiring*.**

___ Helen had a teacher named Annie.
_✓_ Helen became the first deaf and blind person to graduate from college.
_✓_ Helen wrote books and talked with people all over the world.
___ Helen got very sick when she was a year and a half old.

Turn the page.

 95

PROCEDURES

Do not demonstrate or guide practice.

Written Assessment—Basic Instructions

1. Introduce the Written Assessment.
   - Tell students that their work today is an opportunity for them to show what they can do independently. Say something like:
     You should be very proud of your accomplishments. Remember, on a Written Assessment, you get to show me what you can do all by yourself.
   - Tell students they will whisper read the passage and then answer the questions without help.

2. Check for student understanding.
   Say something like:
   Look at your assessment. What are you going to do first? (write my name)

   What are going to do next? (whisper read the passage)
   What will you do after you read the passage? (answer the questions)

   That's great. Now what will you do if you get to a hard question?
   (reread the question and try again)
   That's right. What should you do if it's still hard? (reread the passage and try again)
   Very good. And if you still aren't sure, what will you do? (do my best and keep going)

WRITTEN ASSESSMENT (3 of 3)

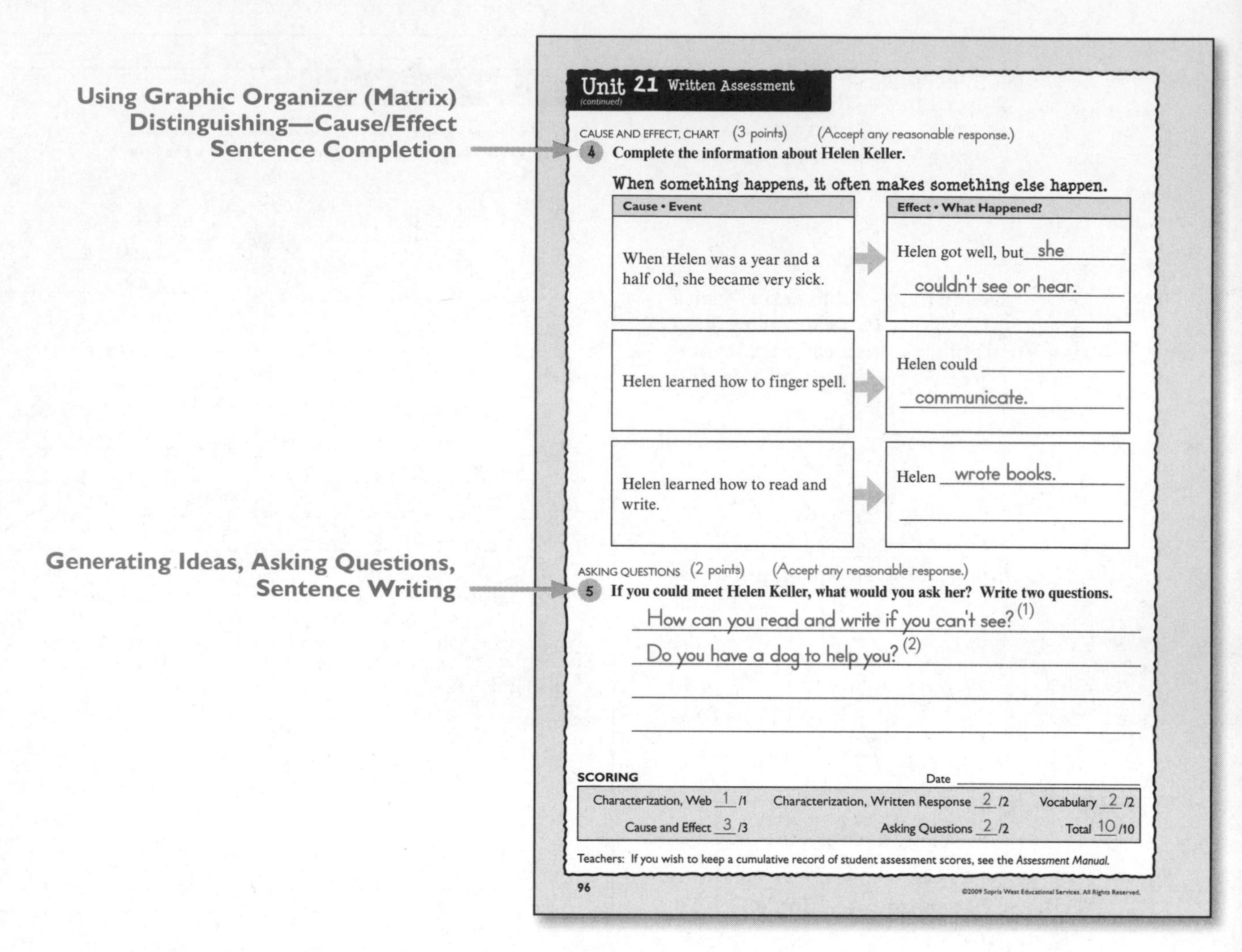

Using Graphic Organizer (Matrix)
Distinguishing—Cause/Effect
Sentence Completion

Generating Ideas, Asking Questions,
Sentence Writing

Unit 21 Written Assessment
(continued)

CAUSE AND EFFECT, CHART (3 points) (Accept any reasonable response.)

4 **Complete the information about Helen Keller.**

When something happens, it often makes something else happen.

Cause • Event	Effect • What Happened?
When Helen was a year and a half old, she became very sick.	Helen got well, but she couldn't see or hear.
Helen learned how to finger spell.	Helen could communicate.
Helen learned how to read and write.	Helen wrote books.

ASKING QUESTIONS (2 points) (Accept any reasonable response.)

5 **If you could meet Helen Keller, what would you ask her? Write two questions.**

How can you read and write if you can't see? (1)

Do you have a dog to help you? (2)

SCORING Date ____________

Characterization, Web 1 /1	Characterization, Written Response 2 /2	Vocabulary 2 /2
Cause and Effect 3 /3	Asking Questions 2 /2	Total 10 /10

Teachers: If you wish to keep a cumulative record of student assessment scores, see the *Assessment Manual.*

96

3. Remind students to check and correct.
   When you finish your assessment, what should you do? (check and correct)
   That's right. Go to the top of the page. Reread the questions and make sure your answers make sense. Fix anything that doesn't sound right. Make sure you have an answer for every question.

4. Remind students what to do when they finish their work.

End of the Unit

In this section, you will find:

Making Decisions

As you near the end of the unit, plan to give the Written Assessment and the Oral Reading Fluency Assessment to each child in your group. Use this section as a general guide for making instructional decisions and doing diagnostic planning.

Written Assessment

The Unit 21 Written Assessment is located on page 93 of *Activity Book 4* and on the blackline master CD.

Oral Reading Fluency Assessment

The Unit 21 Oral Reading Fluency Assessment is located on page 101 and in the *Assessment Manual.*

Certificate of Achievement

Celebrate your children's accomplishments. When your students master the unit skills, send home the Certificate of Achievement.

Making Decisions

GENERAL ASSESSMENT GUIDELINES

1. After students read Story Reading 6, "Changing the Face of History," give the group the Unit 21 Written Assessment in place of Comprehension and Skill Work. Follow the instructions on pages 94–96 of this guide.

2. While the group is completing the Written Assessment or any time during the day, administer the Oral Reading Fluency Assessment. Assess each student individually.

   Optional: Graph the results of the assessment. (See page 100.)
   - If the student's words correct per minute go up, congratulate the student.
   - If the student's words correct per minute go down, discuss the student's overall improvement and help him or her identify ways to improve for the next assessment.

3. Score oral fluency responses on the Student Assessment Record. Adhere to the scoring criteria in the *Assessment Manual.* Use a stopwatch to time how long it takes each student to read the Oral Reading Fluency Passage, and record errors.

USING WRITTEN ASSESSMENT RESULTS

Results of the Written Assessment *should not* be used to determine whether a student or group of students continues forward in the program. As long as students pass the Oral Reading Fluency Assessment, they should continue forward with the next unit.

The Written Assessment should be used to informally monitor how well students read independently and answer questions in writing. If any student has difficulty with the Written Assessment, re-administer the assessment orally.

If the student has difficulty answering the questions orally:
- Record the types of errors (e.g., main idea, sequencing, open-ended response).
- Provide explicit instruction for these types of questions during reading group, before independent work, and in tutorials, as needed.
  1) Demonstrate (or model) appropriate responses, guide practice, and provide opportunities for independent practice.
  2) For inferential questions, think aloud with students—explain how you arrive at an answer.
  3) For literal questions, teach students to reread a passage, locate information, reread the question, and respond.

USING THE ORAL READING FLUENCY RESULTS

At the end of each unit, you will need to make decisions regarding student progress. Should students go forward in the program? Does the group need Extra Practice before proceeding? Do individuals require more assistance and practice to continue working in their group? These decisions all require use of the oral reading fluency data and professional judgment. As you analyze assessment results, watch for trends and anomalies.

See the *Assessment Manual* for detailed information and instructional recommendations. General guidelines and recommendations follow:

Strong Pass ≥ 125 WCPM 0–2 errors	• Continue with the current pace of instruction. • Have students set goals. (Until students are reading approximately 180 words correct per minute, oral reading fluency continues to be an instructional goal.)
Pass 104–124 WCPM 0–2 errors	• Continue with the current pace of instruction. Consider increasing fluency practice.
No Pass ≤ 103 WCPM	• If a child scores a No Pass but has previously passed all assessments, you may wish to advance the student to the next unit, then carefully monitor the student. • If a child scores a No Pass but has previously passed all assessments, you may wish to advance the student to the next unit and also provide additional practice opportunities. (See below.) • If a child scores two consecutive No Passes or periodic No Passes, additional practice must be provided. (See below.) • If a child scores three consecutive No Passes, the student should be placed in a lower-performing group.

RED FLAG

A No Pass is a red flag. A mild early intervention can prevent an intense and time-consuming intervention in the future.

Added Practice Options for Groups

Warm-Ups:

- Begin each lesson with Partner Reading of the previous day's homework.
- Begin each lesson with a five-minute Fluency Booster. Place copies of the Unit 15–20 *Read Well* Homework in three-ring notebooks. Each day, have students begin Finger Tracking and Whisper Reading at Unit 15, Homework 1. At the end of five minutes, have students mark where they are in their notebooks. The next day, the goal is to read farther.
- Begin each Story Reading with a review of the previous day's story.
- After reading the story, include Short Passage Practice on a daily basis.

Jell-Well Reviews: A Jell-Well Review is the *Read Well* term for a review of earlier units. A Jell-Well Review is a period of time taken to celebrate what children have learned and an opportunity to firm up their foundation of learning. To complete a Jell-Well Review, take the group back to the last unit for which all students scored Strong Passes. Then quickly cycle back up. See the *Assessment Manual* for how to build a Jell-Well Review.

Added Practice Options for Individual Students

Tutorials: Set up five-minute tutorials on a daily basis with an assistant, trained volunteer, or cross-age tutor. Have the tutor provide Short Passage Practice and Timed Readings or Extra Practice lessons.

Double Dose: Find ways to provide a double dose of *Read Well* instruction.

- Have the student work in his or her group *and* a lower-performing group.
- Have an instructional assistant, older student, or parent volunteer preview or review lessons.
- Preview new lessons or review previous lessons.

END-OF-THE-UNIT CELEBRATION

When students pass the Oral Reading Fluency Assessment, celebrate with the Certificate of Achievement on page 102.

Note: Using the Flesch-Kincaid Grade Level readability formula, the Unit 21 Assessment has a 3.2 readability level. Readabilities are based on number of words per sentence and number of syllables per word. Adding one or two multisyllabic words can increase readability by a month or two. Though we are attending to readability for the assessments, the overriding factor is decodability.

GRAPHING

You may wish to have students graph their assessment results to enhance motivation and help students monitor their own progress.

- Copy a graph from page 103 for each student and write in students' names.
- For each student, graph the number of words read correctly in Unit 21.
- Explain the graph to students. Say something like:

  I am very proud of all you. Everyone in this group is becoming a more and more powerful reader. You are practicing words. You are practicing stories, and you are becoming fluent readers. Being a fluent reader will help you in fourth grade, eighth grade, high school, and even in college!

  I have a graph for each of you so you see how your reading improves. The first bar tells how many words correct per minute you read on Unit 21.

  When you do your Unit 22 Assessment, we'll fill in the next bar and you can watch your scores climb.

There should be an overall trend of improvement for every child in your group. If an individual student does not show growth from the beginning of the year, intervene immediately.

a. Was the initial placement too high? If yes, the student may need to go back to a more appropriate placement.
b. Is the student reading significantly fewer words correct per minute than others in his or her group? If yes, see the added practice options for individual students.

TRICKY WORD and FOCUS SKILL WARM-UP

borrow	expensive	inspired	neighbor	terrible

ORAL READING FLUENCY PASSAGE

Abe Borrows a Book

★Abraham Lincoln loved to read. One day he heard that 10
a neighbor had a new book. It was called *The Life of George* 23
Washington. Abe walked many miles to borrow the book. The 33
book was expensive, so he promised to return it in good shape. 45

George Washington's life story inspired Lincoln. 51
Washington was a farmer too, and he became the first president 62
of the United States. As Abe read the book, perhaps he thought 74
about becoming president. 77

One night Abe left the book too close to the fire. In the 90
morning the book's cover was burned. Lincoln felt terrible. He 100
would have to tell his friend the truth. He walked back to his 113
friend's farm. 115

Abraham didn't have any money, so he offered to work to 126
pay for the book. He worked on the farm for three days. But at the 141
end of the three days, his friend gave him the book to keep! 154

ORAL READING FLUENCY Start timing at the ★. Mark errors. Make a single slash in the text (/) at 60 seconds. If the student completes the passage in less than 60 seconds, have the student go back to the ★ and continue reading. Make a double slash (//) in the text at 60 seconds.

WCPM Determine words correct per minute by subtracting errors from words read in 60 seconds.

STRONG PASS The student scores no more than 2 errors on the first pass through the passage and reads 125 or more words correct per minute. Proceed to Unit 22.

PASS The student scores no more than 2 errors on the first pass through the passage and reads 104 to 124 words correct per minute. Proceed to Unit 22.

NO PASS The student scores 3 or more errors on the first pass through the passage and/or reads 103 or fewer words correct per minute. Provide added fluency practice. For 2 or 3 days, reteach an exercise page and use a homework passage for fluency practice, then retest.

A Great Reader!

____

has successfully completed

Read Well* 2 Unit 21 • *A Great Man

with ________ words correct per minute.

Teacher Signature __________________________

Date ____________________________________

A Great Reader!

____

has successfully completed

Read Well* 2 Unit 21 • *A Great Man

with ________ words correct per minute.

Teacher Signature __________________________

Date ____________________________________

Name ______________________________ Start Date ____________________

Using a dark pen or marker, fill in the bar to graph the student's score. For any student with a fluency score greater than 180, write his or her score in the top box.

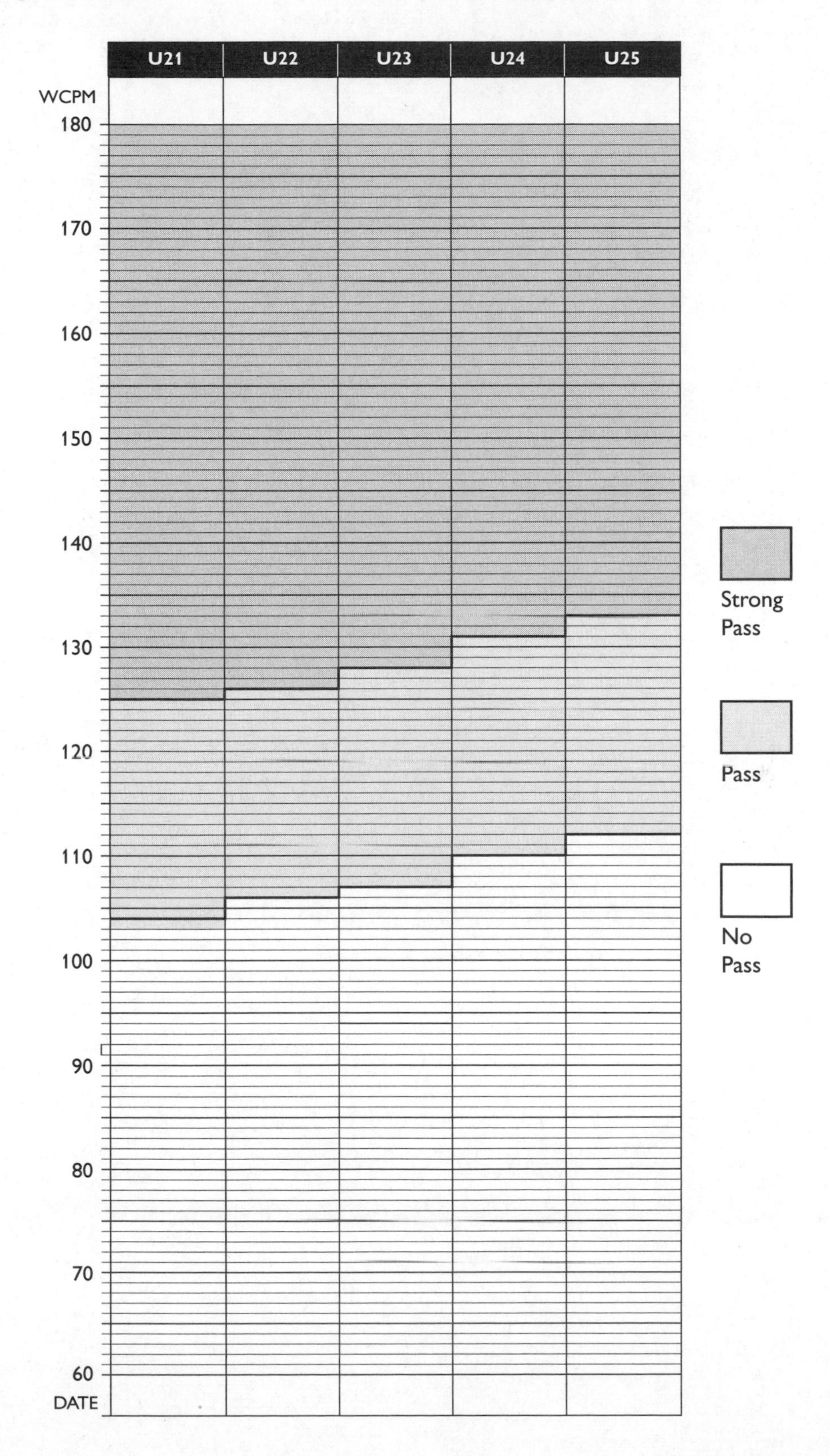